Kill Something and Drag It Home

Robin Bull

Black Moth Publishing – Oklahoma City, Oklahoma

Copyright © 2018 Robin Bull.

All rights reserved. No part of this publication may be reproduced, distributed, or transmitted in any form or by any means, including photocopying, recording, or other electronic or mechanical methods, without the prior written permission of the publisher, except in the case of brief quotations embodied in critical reviews and certain other noncommercial uses permitted by copyright law. For permission requests, write to the publisher use the Facebook page listed below.

ISBN: 9781790439997

Any references to historical events, real people, or real places are used fictitiously. Names, characters, and places are products of the author's imagination.

Front cover image by Robin Bull.

Book design by Robin Bull.

Printed by Black Moth Publishing in the United States of America.

First printing edition 2018.

www.facebook.com/TheRobinBull

Contents

Introduction 4
Section I – It's All in Your Head (Mindset) 8
    No One Else Can Make You Happy 9
    No One Else Can Fix Your Life 11
    What Is Success? 12
A Lesson in the Power of the Mind 14
    Basic Training 14
    Muhammad Ali 15
    Eartha Kitt 17
    You Are What You Think 17
    Making Active Decisions About Your Life 22
    Taking Action to Change Your Life 23
New Habits, New You 25
    Using Positive Affirmations to Change Your Life
    27
Dealing with Imposter Syndrome 31
Turning Your Faults into Assets 34
There's No Such Thing as Competition 37
Section II – Business Management 101 38
    You Have to Do More Than Want It 38
        Rule #1 – Plan Your Work 38
        Rule # 2 – Work Your Plan 42
        Rule #3 – No Excuses 43
Business Plan Basics 45
    Business Goals 48

- Yes, No, Hell No, Maybe 49
- What's for Sale? 53
- Defining the Personality of the Business 53
- Why Would Anyone Hire Me? 55
- Who Are My Customers? 55
- Writing Your Mission Statement 56
- Start-Up Costs 57
- What about More Traditional Business Plans? .. 58
- Executive Summary 59
- Description of Business 60
- Marketing 65
- Appendix 66
- What If You Don't Want a Business Plan at All? 67

- Rate Setting 69
- Can You Really Run a Business from Home with Little Investment? 72
- When Should You Take the Leap? 74
- What about Incorporating? 75
- Scheduling 77
- Understanding Your Target Market 82
- Proposals 85
- No Experience? No Problem! 93
- Marketing 94
  - Free and Next to Free Marketing 96
    - Yes, You Need a Blog 100
  - Content Creation Strategy 103

Email Lists and Digital Downloads	108
Productivity Isn't the Same as Busyness	111
Taxes	112
Should I Sign That?	113
Conclusion	115

Introduction

If anyone could complain about the way life has been, it's me. If anyone has ever had a reason to fail in life, it would be me. I know that most of us could say that, but I can only judge life from my own perspective.

When I was around two years old, my biological father raped me. It's not that someone told me this or that it was repressed memory discovered during therapy. I remember what happened. Even more, I remember my maternal and paternal grandmothers taking me to the doctor and being examined. Guess what? Nothing was ever done about it past that. I was given back to my parents.
A couple of years later, I was diagnosed with ADD (in the 80s, it wasn't as common). I was around four years old. My mother had me placed into a special needs class. She was convinced that there was something more that was wrong with me. It took an IQ test and the dedication of my paternal grandmother to get me out of that class.

We lived in a small town: El Reno, Oklahoma. My brother, Glen, is five years older than I am. When I was four and he was almost nine, we would regularly walk across town alone to our great grandmother's house. I was left unsupervised a lot because our parents were drug addicts and alcoholics. I was frequently found in an area of town known as Rock Island. It was by active railroad tracks. I was most often barefoot, dirty, and hungry. My husband, Danny, and I drove past there a few months back and I was shocked that I could wander so far away and play in such a dangerous area.

When I was five, I was repeatedly molested by two older children that lived across the street from us. My mother walked in on it several times...and did nothing about it. Ever. It was around this time that I recall looking at a clock in the dining room and doing the math to determine exactly how long it would be until I turned 18.

We moved to Oklahoma City when I was eight. I was bullied and beaten up on a regular basis. We moved into an area riddled with drugs and gangs. Again, I was molested by another neighbor.

We moved roughly every six months to a year. I went to 13 different schools. I've had a gun put to my head by other students. I've been sexually assaulted in school. I've been beaten up for being "white." For the record, I'm not white. I'm Native American. My bio dad was extremely dark. I just happened to get my mom's skin coloring. No one should ever be bullied or beaten up for being different.

I went to the worst schools in the state's worst school district. We lived in houses where our windows were shot out. At 15, my mom tried to stab me. She was taken to the Crisis Center by the police and a judge admitted her into a psychiatric facility. She was in and out of mental hospitals because of paranoid schizophrenia. She refused to take her meds as she should and was also abusing other drugs.

There was rarely food in the house. I was routinely asked if I had an eating disorder because I was so thin. No. My parents just chose drugs over buying food.

I got married in 2000 when I was only 22 years old. I had two children. I ignored a lot of red flags with that guy. I knew he was cheating on me. I knew the things he said and did weren't right. He was eventually discharged from the military because of what he said was depression. The military representatives stated to me that they felt he was a threat who had a problem with authority. They kept him locked up for a couple of weeks because they feared for my safety. Still...I stayed. I had this crazy notion of trying to stay in the marriage until the younger son turned 18. The church told me I wasn't praying hard enough. When my oldest son turned 10, the ex dragged me out of bed by my hair. He was drunk. He choked me. All over a picture of my sunburned shoulder that was on Facebook. And still, I stayed.

A couple of times, I got tired of it and left with the kids, but he would threaten to kill our pets. He started cheating on me and told others that I was cheating on him. He stole money from my bank account. He tried to make me crazy through gas lighting. I ended up doing outpatient hospitalization for anxiety and severe depression. One day, both the therapist and the psychiatrist said what I never wanted to admit: I was being abused. The therapist called him with my permission to try to get him to come in and she confronted him. He made me quit counseling and my job.

A couple of years later, he told me that he was leaving me for a young lady who lived across the street from us. I guess she was maybe 19 at the time. We had lived there for 8 years. She was 11 years old when we first moved in. To say I was disgusted was an understatement. I asked and asked for a divorce. He kept saying he would file (because he also kept taking money out of my account). He moved out. She got pregnant. I thought this was no longer my problem and I was so wrong.

I didn't start dating for quite some time, but when I did, he lost it. He began to stalk me. He has software embedded into my laptop so that he could watch me from anywhere. He threatened to send out nude photos he had of me from our marriage. All because I had chosen to go out on a lunch or dinner date when the children weren't with me. One of my sons played football. He choked me out in the car. He followed me everywhere. I had to get a protective order through the state. Eventually, the divorce was granted and he tried to manipulate the system to try and keep the kids from me. When I began teaching college, he tried to get me fired. My mailbox was broken into numerous times. He would sit outside where I lived despite having a girlfriend (that he eventually married). When I remarried, he tried to drag me back to court and alleged that I was committing bigamy…which wasn't true. The divorce was final and he had been living with the same girl for several years. His girl at that time was harassing me, too.

So, why am I telling you all of this? I'm telling you all of this so that you can see the big difference now in my life. And what I have now isn't because I was ever given anything freely in life. As you can see, my life was a relative shit-fest.

Now, I'm in my late 30s. I own a successful professional writing business. I work from home (well, actually, I've rented office space). I started my business while teaching college and working part time in a law firm. I'm happily married. I still deal with PTSD because of my childhood and former marriage, but I don't take any meds for it. Turns out that if you stop surrounding yourself with assholes, your mental state tends to improve. Imagine that. My children are all healthy and happy. I travel with my husband. I work when I want. I enjoy what I do. I have a knack for business.

If anyone had a reason to fail in life, it would be me. I am a product of drug addicts. I am a product of terrible schools. I am a product of childhood, sexual, and domestic abuse. I am all of those things. I also refuse to be broken.

And you can refuse to be broken, too. You can do anything you want in life. You can build a business. You can choose to be successful. It doesn't matter where you came from. Your past doesn't have to be a liability. You can turn it into an asset.

Your power to succeed is all in your mind. Once you make the decision to be successful, you have to follow it up with action. It's not always easy. I still have days where I feel like a failure. I still have days where I function moment by moment. That's just life. The more you take action and begin to think differently, the sooner you will rewire your brain for success.

Section I – It's All in Your Head (Mindset)

Your brain is the most powerful thing in the Universe. With it, you can make your life great or you can make your life a living hell. The power of the mind is absolutely amazing. When you learn how to think differently, even problems seem a little bit easier to solve. Here's the trick in life and business: you are your own biggest problem. You're also the biggest solution.

For my entire childhood and through my first marriage, I was told how worthless and stupid I was. Even after getting out of those situations, my brain took over in telling me those things. Yet, I've taught college. So, I'm clearly far from stupid. I've worked in law firms. I've worked for law schools. I've raised children. I'm clearly not worthless. It wasn't until I decided that I was at least going to try to get what I wanted out of life that I started to see change. And, you'll never see change in your life unless you make a conscious decision to change.

What I am about to say next is going to upset a lot of people. Whether you will fail or succeed is all in your head. It has nothing to do with anyone else. It has nothing to do with your parents. It has nothing to do with your past. It has nothing to do with where you went to school (or whether you went to college). It has to do with you and whether you're willing to put in the work to get there.

No One Else Can Make You Happy

As humans, we are hard wired to want at least some degree of contact with other people. I'm fairly introverted (likely due to my childhood), but even I want some amount of interaction. It's just who we are. There's a reason why people believe that solitary confinement is cruel.
Women, particularly, are molded into thinking that we need something or someone else to make us happy. I don't mean just how many women (including me) have an innate drive to be partnered or to be a mom. I also know women who don't have that desire and that's fine, too. It's just that most of us are raised to think that it will take getting married or having a kid to be happy. We end up with destination addiction. "I will finally be happy when I get married." You get married, then what? "I will finally be happy if I have a baby." Okay, so what happens if you can't have a baby or if you're still not happy after your baby is born? "I'll be happy when I get a job that pays a certain amount of money a year." Then, you figure out that you're really not happy again. Men deal with this, too. It's just part of the human condition.

Yet, no one else can make you happy. No one experience will provide you with a lifetime of happiness. Only you can make you happy. It is an active decision to be content in life. The two major religions of Christianity and Buddhism have reoccurring themes of contentment. Paul says in the New Testament that people should learn to be content regardless of whether they have a little or a lot.[i] Granted, it is easier for people to be content when they don't have to worry about necessities of life. In Buddhism, the main concept is getting rid of attachment. Attachment is more than how you feel about something or someone. It also means that you're not living in the past or constantly worrying about the future. It means that you're being present. You're being mindful.

Mindfulness is one of the best things you can practice to deal with anxiety and depression. I know. I've tried it. I've also tried medications. Mindfulness has been one of the best tools that I've learned that's helped me change my life. Mindfulness sounds incredibly simple, but it can be hard to put into practice for many people. It means that you're present in the here and now. I've used it to deal with panic attacks particularly when I don't know what's triggered it. I work to change my focus. I say things to myself like, "I've felt like this before and I know it does not last forever. I am currently safe." I may even walk through my house and touch things to keep myself grounded into the moment.

Mindfulness can also teach you how to be happy with what you have. If you can't be happy with what you have now, you likely won't be happy no matter what you have in the future. Because you'll always be searching for something else. In conversations with others, mindfulness means that you're actually listening to them instead of thinking of other things or thinking about your response. With your family, it can mean putting down your smartphone and spending time with each other.

Mindfulness doesn't mean that you never think about the past or the future. It just means that you don't dwell on the past and you don't continuously worry about the future. You start to enjoy and appreciate the little things that you have. You might not own your own home, but if you have a roof over your head, that's something to appreciate. You might not eat out in five-star establishments every night, but if you have food in your home, you have something to appreciate.

Your happiness is strictly your responsibility. When you place your happiness on other people, you're creating a problem for yourself and for that relationship. You know deep down that you can't always make someone happy. People can't always make you happy, either. That's a huge emotional responsibility to give to someone else. People are inherently and deeply flawed. You do yourself a huge disservice if you expect others to make you happy.

Learning to be happy requires that you take the time to get to know yourself. It requires that you get to know what you like and what you don't. It also takes you doing things for yourself that you enjoy. It could be as simple as taking an hour each day to indulge in a hobby. It could be buying yourself coffee or reading a book. It could be taking a hot bath and enjoying a glass of wine. Take some time to think about how you can make yourself happy.

Being happy and content in life is a daily decision.

No One Else Can Fix Your Life

Just like no one in the world is responsible for your happiness, no one else can fix your life except for you. The government can't do it (nor should they be trusted to do it). Your spouse can't fix your life. It's not the responsibility of your children. It's not the responsibility of your parents. Going to school is no guarantee of a successful career. Much like how you can't fix someone else's problems, no one else can fix yours. Again, you are your own biggest problem and your own biggest solution.

You must deliberately choose to fix your life. This can mean doing some things that you don't necessarily like. It could mean that you don't do certain things anymore. It could mean that you don't talk to certain people (even family members). It could mean that you must give up time on social media and instead use that time to learn something new that you can use in life.
If you have a money problem, you must fix it. You must find a better job, or you must work two jobs. You can also elect to start your own business. If you have relationship problems, you can try to repair the relationship (but you can't fix crazy and destructive people) or you can get out of the relationship. I stopped talking to my biological father

about three years before he died. I was tired of being a scapegoat. I am strictly no contact with the ex-husband. When the children were minors, wasn't particularly easy, but that's why courts and lawyers were involved. And any time that I communicated with him, it was done by text message so that it was documented in writing.

As of 2016, for profit colleges are getting shut down left and right. This is leaving tons of students and faculty in a bad spot. Many students maxed out their financial aid and ended up with credits that won't even transfer to a local community college. That's a bad situation to be in, but no one can fix it for them. They can apply to have their loans forgiven, but it doesn't make up for the time that they feel they wasted since many of them won't even receive the degree that they were promised.

There are no guarantees in life. When we have issues, we must fix them on our own. Ultimately, whether we succeed or fail is up to us. Sometimes that means making the best out of a bad situation. And to be able to do that, we have to learn how to think differently. That's why I've said that your brain is the most powerful tool you own.

What Is Success?

The problem with defining success is that it can be different for everyone. So, you must look at it more as what you would consider successful. How do you know if you've had a successful day? What about a successful week? Month? Year?

Success changes over time. I consider success now as continuing to be able to provide for my family and to not be miserable during the process. I have an office. I have clients. There is food in my kitchen. My bills are paid. I can pretty much do whatever I want during the day. That's success for me right now.

There was a time, though, when success for me was getting out of a bad marriage in one piece. It was having the money to keep the electricity on.

So, what's success for you? You must think of success in two ways. You have your short-term successes and your long-term successes. A short-term success is something that you could accomplish in the next month or two. The long-term success is something you could accomplish in the next year. No one can define success for you...only you can do that. Success is all about personal responsibility.

Take some time to think about what you would consider success. Get a notebook and start writing down your goals. Then, add some dates by them. Give each goal its own page. Break down what you have to do to make that goal into your reality. Goals are only dreams unless you have a plan.

A plan does you no good unless you take action.

A Lesson in the Power of the Mind

To show you just how powerful the mind truly is, let's look at a few examples.

Basic Training

Do you know anyone that's ever been in the military? We have one of the most admired militaries in the world. A lot of that has to do with the fact that it is a voluntary process. Yes, we have a draft, but it's not used. Rather, people volunteer to go to basic training and be yelled at and put down for several weeks. They are first broken down so that they can be built up into members of the world's most admired military. People who make it through the basic training process come out as a totally different person on the other side. They are more self-confident. They're more physically fit. They're soldiers. That is the power of the mind.

Maybe you spent most of your life being yelled at, screamed at, insulted, or even beaten. It does break you down. It makes you feel like less of a person...or that maybe you're not even a person at all. It's a tough spot to be in. Yet, there are plants that bloom in the desert. There's a saying about people who go through extremely hard times and they come out from the other side: They tried to bury us, but they did not know that are seeds.

Unlike someone who volunteers for the process of going to basic training, you didn't volunteer for that treatment. Yet, you endured it. You've been broken down. Once that happens, you must find a way to build yourself back up.

Fortunately, you don't have to rely on a government representative to determine how best to build you up.

Nope. You might think it's some sort of disaster that you don't have anyone to rebuild you. You get the opportunity to build yourself back into being anything you want. Let that sink in.

You can be the person that you've always dreamed of being. You can be more confident. You can be the person that experiences self-love. You can pretty much re-design your entire life to include any traits you've always wanted to have...with maybe the exception of growing taller!

You get to retrain your mind. It's not easy, but it's an exciting prospect. You will have days where you feel like a fake. You will have days where you feel great. It's all a process. One day, you'll wake up and just be who you've designed yourself to be.

This can be difficult for many people. Those of us that were told for entire lives how worthless and stupid we are certainly continue to say that about ourselves long after we are no longer around the person or persons who said those things to us. We continue to repeat those things in our own head because the time we spent hearing it literally rewired our brains. We've made self-fulfilling prophecies. Because we believe the break down that was given to us, we continue to repeat it...and live it.

The good news is that you can change it. Before we move on and discuss how you can do that, let's look at another example of the power of the mind.

Muhammad Ali

Muhammad Ali, born as Cassius Clay Jr., is likely the best example in the world when it comes to seeing just how powerful our mind is. Even better, Ali backed up his self-talk with action. That's a core principle of building yourself back up and becoming the person that you want to be. Ali literally took on a new identity. Although, we should keep in mind that his name change came about from his religious conviction. Yet, unlike many others of his time and even people today, he backed up his beliefs with action.

Many felt that Ali was absolutely brash for his self-proclamation of being the greatest. They put him down for his religious convictions. He stood against the war and even spent time behind bars because of it. He was outspoken. He lived his life out loud. He did not hide behind others.

Ali went from being a black man born during a time of great racial tension to being one of the most celebrated boxers and activists of all time. Even after his death, there are people that still don't like him. There are people who practically worship him.

It's important to ask yourself how you want to be remembered after your death. It's also important to ask yourself how you want to live your life now. Regardless of how you feel or felt about Ali, one thing is for sure. He was best at self-promotion. His comments and his actions always kept him the talk of the town. Ali was a display of power. He was a display of confidence. Most importantly, he was a display of hope to people that regardless of where they came from and how they were being oppressed, they could rise above and be successful.

Ali also used the attention he received to address injustice. He addressed the very injustice that he faced as a black man of the time. Think about what injustice you would speak out against if you were to rise to power. Wouldn't having your voice heard and having the ability to call attention to that injustice be worth the struggle to get there? If you could change just one life by speaking up, would you?

Eartha Kitt

It makes no difference where you come from. I'm a product of drug addicts and I managed to become a success. Eartha Kitt, a talented actress and singer, was a product of rape. She was raised by an aunt that she believed was her biological mother. Catwoman, despite having a past that her mind could have used to hold herself back, was anything but a failure. She was even called the most exciting woman in the world by Orson Welles.

Kitt had two #1 radio hits. She was a movie star. She was a little girl who lived with her aunt and then who was sent to live with her biological mother (that she didn't even know at the time). She was and is a celebrated inspiration who continues to show all of us that where we come from in life and even the hardships we suffer aren't nearly as important as what we choose to do.

Life is all about making a choice. Kitt did not whine and complain about her upbringing or how she was brought into this world. She did not spend her life wallowing in self-pity because she was sent to live with her aunt who later shipped her off to her birth mother. No. She went out and made her life into what she wanted it to be.

In fact, Kitt started Kittsville Youth Foundation, a non-profit for underprivileged children. Yet again, another shining example of someone with a less than settled upbringing who not only went on to find success, but also did things to make the world a better place.

Upon Kitt's death, her daughter is quoted as saying, "...she left this life with a bang, she left it as she lived it."

You Are What You Think

It may sound cliché, but there is no bigger truth than this. You are what you think. If you think that you're a good and successful person, you'll begin to do the things good and successful people do. If you think that you can't accomplish anything in life, you'll take on a self-fulfilling prophecy and you'll either sabotage yourself or you simply won't try.

What you think about yourself and your life is the most important tool you must create the life that you want. While this is a simple revelation, it is much more difficult to accept and begin to live by. All too often we find ourselves drowning in a sea of unruly thoughts. Even once you accept that you are what you think and begin to work toward changing your thoughts, you'll still have times where it is incredibly hard to do. Changing the way that you think about yourself, your success, and your life is an active process. It is something that we do every day. It is something that requires mindfulness. In a society that loves to jump from one activity and one thought to another in the name of productivity (and no, multitasking does not make you more productive – it makes you prone to make more mistakes), it can be hard to be mindful.

First, you must be mindful of negativity. There will always be negativity on this planet. There will always be bad news. There will always be negative people…and sometimes those people are your friends and family. Frankly, I am a firm believer that you can't have anything positive without some negativity because you wouldn't ever appreciate the positive aspects. We'd get used to them and they'd stop affecting us. It is really, really hard to begin a journey toward being self-positive if your brain is full of the negative. The simplistic answer is to stay away from as much negativity as possible. That can be hard to do, but if you want your life to change, you must change.

Next, begin to remove negativity from your life. We're going to look at this in two ways: external negativity and internal negativity. External negativity is anything outside of you that is negative. It could be an overabundance of negativity on television or radio. It could be your friends or family. With external negativity, it's both easy and hard to deal with. It's easy because controlling what you expose yourself to on purpose is within your control. You can turn off the television. You can turn off the radio. You can read a book. I promise you that you're not going to turn into some hermit who doesn't know a damn thing about the world. You'll be in the know. People never shut up. The point isn't to be uneducated about the happenings in the world. It's about making room in your brain for things that can change your life. If you love to listen to the news or talk radio, you have options. You can listen to other podcasts. In fact, you should find and listen to podcasts that will help you be a better you. Spotify, Podbean, BlogTalkRadio, and other websites are devoted to podcasts. And most of them are free.

Another external negativity factor is people in your life. I was 24 when I cut my biological father out of my life for good. He died the next year…shortly after my 25th birthday. While it may be awful to think that an adult child had nothing to do with a parent the year before they died, it does show you the importance of creating room for peace and positivity in your life. You are under no obligation to keep negative people in your life. And I know you thought of at least one person in your family or at least one of your friends when you read that. You can block them on social media. You can block them from your phone. You do not have to keep people like that in your life. Your life should be peaceful.

Will you feel guilty when you cut people out of your life? It's a possibility. Again, though, you're under absolutely no obligation to keep negative people in your life regardless of whether you are related to them. Guilt is a feeling that you should reserve for when you actually do something wrong. Cutting people out of your life is a choice you are entitled to make. You're not going to necessarily end up as a recluse living in a cave by the sea. You're going to think about the qualities you want in a friend and those are the type of people that you should begin to gravitate toward in order to build relationships. You'll have less drama in your life and more peace.

Then, we learn to deal with internal negativity. Where does this internal negativity come from? We aren't born hating ourselves. It comes from what others say to us and how they treat us. It comes from the media. It comes from society as a whole. It comes from mixed messages. Think about how often women are told to love themselves just as they are. Yet, all of the advertisements on television do nothing but tell us how we are flawed and need to look better in some way. We're set up for failure because we're told to be great moms, great spouses, great housekeepers, and have fantastic careers. Sorry – you only get 24 hours in a day. The superwoman mentality could drive you crazy and make you feel incompetent. Oh, and if you do love yourself? If you do find yourself attractive? If you do think you're smart? If you own up to being happy with yourself? The most common response you'll hear is, "No you're not. How dare you love you. You're awful for thinking highly of yourself."

I say this a lot. If you grow up hearing that you're stupid, ugly, and won't ever amount to anything, those thoughts won't stop when you become an adult even if you get away from the person or people who say those things to you. Hearing those things all the time will rewire your brain. That's not just my opinion. It's a fact. It's how we learn many things in life – through repetition. Unfortunately, with this aspect, we're not learning the truth. We're not learning anything of value. We're being drilled with another person's perception. Even when that person is gone, our brains keep repeating what it heard for so long. Just like children learn sight words when they first begin to read, we've memorized this behavior.

If you've ever tried to break a bad habit, you know just how hard it is to change. In this case, it's not even that we're breaking a bad habit so much as we are taking control over our brains. That's really hard to do. It takes cultivating mindfulness, a willingness to feel stupid at first (I know I did), and just continuing on even if we don't think that we're getting anywhere with it.

Most major belief systems have a saying of some kind about controlling your thoughts. One of the best known Bible verses related to this (and there are more) is Philippians 4:8 - ...whatever is true, whatever is noble, whatever is right, whatever is pure, whatever is lovely, whatever is admirable – if anything is excellent or praiseworthy – think on those things.

Not Christian? No problem. Buddha stated that we should have right thoughts (and right words). "All that we are is the result of what we have thought. If a man speaks or acts with an evil thought, pain follows him. If a man speaks or acts with a pure thought, happiness follows him, like a shadow that never leaves him."

Even the Prophet Muhammad had a little something to say about controlling our thoughts. "Whoever believes in Allah and the Last Day, let him speak goodness or remain silent."

Of course, you don't need a belief system to experience the power involved in getting negative thoughts out of your head. Learning to think better about yourself and to improve your thought quality has nothing to do with a religious reward. It has everything to do with improving your quality of life.

So, then, what do we do? When you say to yourself that you're dumb, ugly, stupid, worthless, or anything else that's negative, stop that thought. Replace it. You don't have to go overboard and declare that you're the best ever at whatever it is, but you can talk better about it to yourself. If you made a mistake, own it. You can say, "I made a mistake when I was doing X, but I learned from it and I will do better next time. I tried and did the best that I could." If you find yourself verbally berating yourself and telling yourself that you're not worthy of a good life, stop that thought and definitely say the exact opposite. "I am not stupid. I am smart. I am worthy of happiness, success, and love." And, yes, again, there is a possibility that you're going to feel extremely strange.

It takes time, but eventually you will have fewer negative thoughts about yourself. You'll begin to feel more confident. You'll have more success in life. You'll be at peace with yourself. When you are at peace with yourself, it's crazy how much of the world you can experience.

Stopping those thoughts is key, though. It's mindfulness. It is both simple (in theory) and hard (in practice). You will not be a failure if you don't do it every time. However, the more you remember to do it, especially when it is hard, the better results you will have.

Making Active Decisions About Your Life

As you've seen, life is very much about making active decisions. If you decide that you don't want to do anything with life but float along, that's still making a decision. If you don't make the decision to act to change your life, nothing will change. The definition of insanity is doing the same thing over and over again and expecting a different result.

If you want happiness, you must make that decision. Then, you must act. It's not a "one and done" routine, either. If you want success, you must make the decision to be successful. You must know how you will define success. You can't sit around and wait for it to fall into your lap. You must take action toward it.

Life isn't for bystanders. You're only going to get one. Even if you're a believer of reincarnation, you're here now and you might as well make the best of it. Yet, to make the best of it you must decide that's what you want to do.

Unfortunately, when it comes to deciding to take control over their life, people often say that they're afraid. The question is what about that scares you? Is it the fear of failure? No one is perfect. Everyone fails. Look up famous authors like Stephen King and read about the many rejection letters received by agents and publishing houses. Too often, people are more afraid of success. They won't know what to do when they get it. My suggestion is to cross that bridge when you get there...because once you get there, you'll set new goals to further your success.
So, what decisions are you going to make about your life? What do you want to get out of it?

Taking Action to Change Your Life

Of course, making a decision isn't enough. I could decide that I want to be a runway model, but I won't wake up tomorrow at the right height. I could decide that I want to be a millionaire, but tomorrow when I wake up, I can't run out and buy five brand new cars. Decisions are a step in the right direction, but they aren't enough on their own.

Rather, you must take action each and every day in order to achieve the goals that you set. If you decide that you want to live a happier life, then you must do things each day that make you feel that way. You must choose to act a certain way. That's not to minimize chemical depression or anxiety disorders. I deal with anxiety each and every day. It is to say that we can still choose to do something. It may be hard, but we can do it.

That's the next point. You must take action even when you don't feel like it. Hard days, easy days...doesn't matter. If you want to be successful in life and in business, you must take action. There will certainly be some days where you want to give up. Everyone has those days. Successful people push through it. It's about acknowledging that it's hard and choosing to do it anyway.

I don't want to get up every day and work. There are some days I don't want to do anything except sleep. Throughout my life, I've learned that the entire battle is showing up and getting started. In the Business 101 section, you'll learn some techniques that you can use to make decisions and act even on days that totally suck. I've found that when I am able to make a plan and execute on it, how my day feels to me doesn't matter. The actions I take will determine the outcome. Whatever you want for tomorrow, next week, next month, and next year you must start working toward right now.

New Habits, New You

I am a firm believer that there is very little in life that is more difficult than changing a habit. You have to drop some habits in order to develop new habits. By new habits, I mean new actions that will lead you the life that you want to live. I know it's hard. I had to do it.

I suppose I truly started my journey to changing my entire life about five years ago. That's because up until that point, I felt like my life was pretty much hopeless...like I was stuck. So stuck, in fact, that during the last marriage and then two years after it ended, I was diagnosed with Complex PTSD. One of the differentiating factors between PTSD and Complex PTSD is that with Complex PTSD, your brain essentially tells you that you are forever stuck where you are. There is no chance of getting out of it. Nothing will ever change. It's an extremely despondent diagnosis because it's not so much as having occasional flashbacks, nightmares, hyper-vigilance, and the likes. No. You constantly live in that state. So, when I say I know how hard it is to change, I mean it. When I decided I had enough of always feeling like that, I was scared because I had no idea if I was capable of change. I knew it would be hard, but I didn't know just how hard.

So, how did I start? I started by learning how to talk to myself differently. The main reason why most of us get stuck in life is because after other people stop verbally abusing us, our brain takes over. When my brain would start up, I would immediately say the opposite, and often I would say it out loud or whisper it to myself. My goal was to interrupt the thought. This was probably one of the hardest things I had to do. It's something I still occasionally fight with because it is so ingrained into me. I started looking up ways to deal with my thought process and anxiety. I felt really stupid sitting in my living room going through guided meditations for anxiety, but you know what? With time not only did it stop feeling so stupid, but I started to see results. Regardless of your religious affiliation (or lack thereof), meditation is a wonderful tool. It's not about controlling your thoughts so much as it is about learning to let go of them.

I started taking the time to do things that I wanted to do. It was a little hard to go back to some of my old hobbies that I loved. My brain still associated them with ridiculous fights with the ex. They had a lot of negative feelings associated with them. So, I would only work on them for short periods and I would have to combat those thoughts and remind myself I am not in that situation. Another issue was that my brain would kick off the, "You don't have time to do things you like. You need to do the dishes. You need to do the laundry. You should be busy working. You're just wasting time." That's one I still struggle with because I am a big proponent of being industrious. Yet, there's a lot of studies that show that taking some down time is actually good for your mental health and your productivity.

Those aren't the only habits I had to teach myself. I had to teach myself to be more confident. I had to teach myself to speak up for what was right. I had to teach myself that I was a capable business person. All of these habits (and all of the others I eventually picked up related to how I run my business) started because I figured out what I wanted to be and how I wanted others to see me. Then, I started reading. First, I located people that had traits that I wanted to have. I started reading articles written about them or by them. Next, I started reading a lot of self-help books. I spent a lot of time at the library,

I also had to learn about how habits are formed. It takes around 30 days to form a new habit. It's not always an easy 30 days, either. If you wanted to stop procrastinating, you would have to act on something every time you felt the urge to procrastinate. As you can image, that would be really hard. So, you must come up with a way to reward yourself. Your reward doesn't have to be big. It doesn't even have to cost you money. It could be a new soap that you like. It could be indulging in a hobby. It could be just giving yourself permission to rest.

You also have to condition yourself.

Using Positive Affirmations to Change Your Life

I can't say enough good things about the use of positive affirmations to reprogram your brain. Really. Most people who know me would call me a hard ass in many respects. I am highly logical. I prefer facts. I'm just sort of "It is what it is" and that's what you deal with. Yet, it got to a point for me after the first marriage that I just couldn't seem to get out of my own head. My biological father had died several years before and I had been out of the marriage for a couple of years...and yet, their words consumed my brain. It didn't matter that I was teaching law courses for paralegals. I was dealing with something I call "auto-play" brain.

My bio parents weren't good people. Nothing I ever did was good enough. I wasn't smart enough. I wasn't pretty enough. I would never be good for anything. I was stupid. I was a slut. I was destined to be a drug addict (for the record, I've never done drugs – that was their projection of their habits onto me).

I kept trying really hard in school. I did well. My teachers praised me (which helped, I'm sure). My grandmother, aunt, and uncle always had something positive say at report card time (to be fair, my grandmother and aunt were always kind to me...my uncle? I don't think he meant to be a dick, but he was very gruff...however, when I struggled in school, he did everything he could to tutor me and to get me the help I needed at his own expense of money and time).

Even after I got married, that didn't change. My parents called a lot to tell me how awful and worthless I was as a daughter, a mother, a wife, and a human. The ex wasn't much better. Despite working full time, caring for the older boys (I did not go back to work full time until they were school age), and doing well in college, he considered me a terrible person as well. I was dragged out of bed by my hair. He cheated on me and then told everyone that I was the one out cheating. I got text messages on my way to work OT on Saturdays (even when the children went with me) that he knew I was really going out to meet some guy. He choked me. He tried to get me to kill myself.

And after we weren't together? And even years after my biological father died and I limited contact with my mother? My thoughts were on auto-play: worthless. Awful. Stupid. Bad person. Things that I knew from a logical perspective couldn't be true. I did everything I could for everyone (even when I shouldn't). I had a therapist tell me I was co-dependent. I told her no…it wasn't co-dependency (my mother was and is co-dependent). Mine was a moral drive to lessen the suffering of others. I wasn't a bad person. My brain was wired to repeat the nonsense I heard for most of my life.

It took me a long time to accept something that I tell other people quite a bit: you are what you think. If you want to change your life, you must change your thoughts. It's a simple concept, but it's hard to do.

It's easy to say just don't think those things about yourself. It's another thing to actually do it. It's not easy because it is so ingrained into who we are. I had to learn to hit the stop button. If you've ever tried to break a habit or even make a new habit, you know that you must remain cognizant and force yourself to take the right actions. You must use willpower and you have to do things even when it is hard.

I learned to hit the stop button on those thoughts by taking my thoughts captive. There are roughly 25 Bible verses about your thoughts. There are Buddhist verses regarding thoughts. There are Islamic verses as well. All of them boil down to take control over what you let into your mind and focus on the good.

The problem was despite the fact I taught college, despite the fact my sons loved me (then and they love me now – ha!), even though I eventually remarried an amazing man…the thoughts didn't go away. And I felt like they were true (emotionally, not logically – because you know when you're doing the right things in your life and for others, you're not a bad person).

Sometimes, when we're trying to break a bad habit, we struggle because we don't have anything to replace it with. When I was a child, there was an old man in the neighborhood who carried Dum Dum suckers in his front pocket. They weren't for us children. I asked him about it when I was about 11: *why do you carry so many suckers?* He said it was because he stopped smoking and having the suckers gave him something to do with his fingers (reach into the shirt pocket where he used to keep cigarettes) and his mouth. He'd done it for around 15 years at that point. He was sure that was the only reason he was able to quit smoking. Of course, we could debate whether all that sugar as good for him, but the point is – he replaced a killer habit with something less likely to kill him. I bet when he first started, he felt stupid….a grown ass man (in the late 80s) who was probably in his 60s walking around with a sucker in his mouth. In our neighborhood, that wasn't a common sight. Come to think of it, in our neighborhood, I probably shouldn't have been talking to strangers…

Anyway…

So, when I'd notice one of those thoughts starting, I stopped it as soon as I recognized it. Then, I said the exact opposite to myself. And at first, I didn't believe that I was good, smart, or talented. I felt like a fraud. But I kept doing it because it had a purpose.

To reinforce what I was doing to change my thoughts, I added positive affirmations. They don't have to be outlandish. They can be simple. I actually used Buddhist positive affirmations that I found online. They were statements like 'I am peace.' I found it years ago online.

I said them to myself in the morning before I left to teach. I said them in the evening. Just like with stopping the negative thoughts and replacing them with better thoughts, I felt kind of silly at first with the positive affirmations. But....something wonderful happened. Over time, I became more peaceful toward myself. I began to love myself. I began to see my worth.

There are tons of websites that are devoted to positive affirmations. You can find affirmations about anything that you'd like. You can even use binaural beats that have subliminal ideas about creating wealth and success. The key is to find the ones that best speak to you and to your goals...and to actually use the process for a length of time. I still use both positive affirmations and binaural beats.

Dealing with Imposter Syndrome

At some point, maybe even where you currently are in life, you think about where you are and where you want to be. And how you're going to get there. Your life is a combination of your beliefs, your decisions, and your actions. So, what you believe, what you decide, and what you do should have one ultimate goal: getting you where you want to be. During the process, and even when you meet your goal, you could deal with imposter syndrome. You know, feeling like you don't belong or feeling like you've done nothing to deserve the life you aimed to have. So, let's talk about how to deal with it.

First, you must understand that everyone goes through this at some point. It's highly likely you'll deal with it more than once. I still go through it from time to time. It's just part of life. It doesn't mean that you're a fraud. It doesn't mean you suck. It doesn't mean you screwed up. It doesn't mean that you didn't do enough. It just is. You can thank society for that, really. We're all told to go after our dreams. Yet, when we do, there's often little (or no) support. When success occurs? We usually don't have the same friends. We're called sell-outs, snobs, bitches, and everything under the sun. So, yes, imposter syndrome is often just part of the price we pay for success.

Next, you must address your global beliefs. Global beliefs are beliefs that affect the totality of your life. I'm sure you've heard the concept of self-fulfilling prophecy. You think something about yourself long enough, you start to believe it. When you believe it, you'll likely act on it. You must make sure that you don't have some sort of global belief about being a failure that you haven't addressed. It could be that you don't feel as if you deserve success (likely because one or more persons told you that for a portion, or all, of your life). It could be that you're afraid of success.

Let's face it – while success is nice, we often don't think about the proverbial other side of the coin. We think about the nice things – more money means paying bills and maybe owning a few (or a lot) of nice things. What we rarely consider (until we get there) is the negative side of success. You might lose friends. Don't forget the potential of a more complicated tax situation. More publicity. More rumors. More stress. So, many people hold a global belief of being afraid of success. They may not think about the money or the rumors, but they damn sure think about the stress and the possibility of losing friends.

And can we talk about the people who talk shit for just a minute? For the most part, I've always projected an air of confidence...or crazy...depending on who you ask. As a young teen and young adult, I realized that resting bitch face combined with a no bullshit tone of voice saved me from a lot of problems. Most people just left me alone. Those who didn't would realize pretty quick that I was not someone to be trifled with. You know, kinda like a puffer fish (except I've always held the physical ability to protect myself).

Just a few years back, I was not invited to a family wedding. That really didn't bother me. Someone who was invited to the wedding that I'm related to by marriage decided to take it upon themselves to attempt (keyword) a verbal assault on me via social media. I was told that because I change my hair color (and have pretty regularly since high school) that I'm a fraud and don't know who I am. Well, okay then.

Here's the thing about people who talk shit. They're bored. They're jealous. They hate their life and they want you to hate yours. Have you ever met someone who was publicly hateful toward someone who was doing better than the subject of their venom-laced word vomit? Of course not. There's a reason why they don't like you. And that reason is because they hate that you have the courage to do something with your life.

The problem with shit talkers is that if you're still not in a place where you're becoming more comfortable with who you are, it can throw you for a loop. It can cause you to re-embrace the negative self-talk and loathing I'm teaching you to avoid. It can cause you to question yourself and what you're doing. Don't. As time goes on, you'll learn that those who are successful have little time to attack anyone who is looking to change for the better. They know what it's like to make the change. They're glad to see someone do something in life. And that brings me to my third point.

Surround yourself with people who you want to be like. This isn't first grade. Unless you're pulling the proverbial "single-white-female" maneuver, no one who has the values you want to adopt will really object to you emulating them. It's extremely helpful to surround yourself with people you want to be like because it reinforces what you're doing. It helps you continue down the right path. It can also act as a valuable network in the future.

Here's the "too long, didn't read" version: don't stop just because you feel like you're an imposter. Address why you feel that way. Remember that people who talk shit hate their own lives. Create a network of like-minded people with skills and values you want to emulate.

Turning Your Faults into Assets

I've been called neurotic and moderately obsessive since I was a child. I'm a chronic insomniac. The downside is that I'm always tired. The upside is that I have more time in my day to complete tasks than most people. If you are a chronic insomniac, I don't necessarily recommend that you schedule things when you should at least be trying to sleep. What I am saying is that if you can't sleep, be productive.

Have you been called a perfectionist? A cynic? A negative nelly who finds the problem in every good idea? Good news, my friend, those things can be assets...if you choose to use those things in that way. Again, we're back to looking at changing how we think...how we perceive.

I have C-PTSD and ADHD. Both of those mean I have some odd characteristics. Here's my positive spin associated with some of them:

- **Hyper-vigilance.** Hyper-vigilance is a state of mind that means I am constantly on alert. It's a little bit like a compulsion because I might constantly check my pocket to make sure I have my bank card (knowing damn well that I do). It also makes me extremely alert to what is going on around me. When I taught college, we had to undergo active shooter training. Our tiny college had a strange shape. While people were only supposed to go through the doors near reception, there were other unlocked doors in the building. I was able to walk security and the Campus Director through and show them their biggest issues and how someone could get in the building without being detected. Hyper-vigilance means I think about things in a way that most people don't. I'm an excellent analyst and great at-risk management. I think ahead.

- **Anxiety.** It may not sound like a strength, but it can be. So, how could constantly worrying about everything be a strength? Because it changes the way I think. I can consider projects from all angles, note the particular areas where problems may occur, and have a plan for those issues. Proper planning prevents piss poor performance.

- **Moderately obsessive about time.** Because of my moderate obsession with time (I don't sleep in a room where a clock is visible), I am excellent at time management and project management. I know how to make the most of every minute I have in every day. I carefully record the time I spend on various projects so that I am able to give accurate time estimates.

- **Neurotic tendencies.** If there's one thing about me that most people notice if they spend a lot of time with me, it would be that I like my days to follow certain patterns. I don't care so much about doing things at exact times. I can be very meticulous when it comes to planning my work day (and even my own spare time). This means I am a great project manager. Nothing gets missed. I check and re-check what needs to be done along with the quality of the work.

- **Overachiever.** I used to be given such shit as a child and in the corporate world because of my overachieving ways. I can't help it that my brain is faster than the brains of most people. Being an overachiever in business helps me in two distinct ways: it means I get paid more on flat rate projects because I do them faster. It also means that my clients get more than they bargained for and come back again and again. It's like a client care goldmine.

- **Easily distracted.** Always have been, probably always will be. How is this an asset? Because generally when I get distracted, it's because the idea the client presents makes me think of other things that they could benefit from.

- **Hyper-focus.** When someone gets easily distracted on some items and yet zeroes in on others to the point that the world fades away, that's a trait of ADHD. I get so focused on my work that the rest of the world tends to just disappear. I just tune everything out. For clients, this is great because who doesn't want their contractor to have all of their focus on their project?

Stop thinking of your personal faults as a liability. Learn how to turn them into an asset. I can't do it for you, but I do hope that reading about how I see and utilize my quirks can help you.

There's No Such Thing as Competition

When it comes to business, I have a unique outlook. I don't necessarily believe in the concept of competition. It doesn't bother me that there are other people who write books, web content for lawyers, or whatever. It just doesn't matter to me. I don't see them as competitors. It doesn't matter if they make more money than I do. I'll answer questions from aspiring freelance writers because I know that most of them will never bother to act on their plans...or they will quit when they realize it's hard work.

If you're able to stop viewing everyone in your industry as competition, you'll be much happier. If you can't, keep in mind that you need friends or acquaintances in your industry. You need people that you can refer out to if you can't help someone. People in your industry aren't competition. They are a goldmine of information. The websites and blogs of established industry professionals can give you great insight about what your target market wants to read about. You should never, ever, ever steal another person's work. You can and should use their ideas as inspiration for your own.

There are industry websites ran by associated organizations that list averaged prices. This is important if you're going into a creative field of some kind. You need to know what the standard rates are for experienced and not so experienced people. You'll learn more about setting your rate in the Section II, but it's important that you do your research.

When you offer the gold standard in client care, you don't have competition. Although we live in a time where people want instant solutions, we all want excellent customer service. Answering questions through social media, quick email reply times, and going above and beyond are ways that you can impress clients and keep them coming back to you.

Section II – Business Management 101

You Have to Do More Than Want It

I have three rules that result in a successful business. I've been asked many times why I share my exact formula for running a business and why I give out free business advice. The answer to both questions is the same. I don't really lose anything by sharing this information (except maybe a few minutes of my time). It doesn't create 'competition' for me. The fact is that I could hold someone's hand and teach them everything I know about business, but although I am successful, there's no guarantee that they will be successful...because the chance that they will actually buckle down and put in the work is pretty much zero. People want to be successful. They want the "lifestyle." What they don't want is the work and the commitment it takes to create and maintain it. People just don't want to work. So, when I share information, that's all it is...sharing information. Then people say to themselves, "Man, that's hard. I don't wanna give up this or that. That takes too much time."

Where your attention and work is placed, that's what will affect your life. Not everyone is cut out to be self-employed. That's just fact. If someone can't manage their time, work on their own, and learn how to meet (and exceed) the needs of their clients, they won't be successful.

Rule #1 – Plan Your Work

Planning is one step further than dreaming. It means you're writing things down. It means that you're doing the necessary research on your industry. It means that you have a business plan. Once you have your business, it means that each and every day you know what you need to do...everything from client work to marketing to business administration (that's a fancy way of saying paperwork).

Each morning when I get up, I have a specific routine. First, I get into the right mindset. How you get into the business mindset will be up to you. For me, it's a combination of things. It usually includes a guided meditation and binaural beats related to creativity, focus, and anxiety relief. I am a member of a gym and I also live very close to parks that have walking paths. Exercise is extremely important for entrepreneurs. That's not just my opinion, either[ii]. Seriously, though, you shouldn't just take my word for it. Exercise every day for a month and watch how it improves your brain. You could experience fewer mood swings and even have more energy and focus. Sometimes, I check my email while I'm on a treadmill and sometimes I don't. I can tell you, though, that there is a distinct difference in the way I function when I am faithful to both meditation and exercise.

I get dressed. Some days it's just jeans or shorts and a t-shirt. Other days, I'll dress nice even if I don't have anywhere to go or any video conferences scheduled. The better you feel like you look, the better you will feel[iii]. The better you feel, the more you love what you do. For me, it helps prevent burnout. Preventing burnout is part of my overall plan for world domination.

Sometimes, I do a chore or two around the house before I start work. For me, a tidy space helps me focus on my client work. Sometimes, I have to restrain myself from my own tendencies to make sure everything is done. I like things done a certain way. However, one struggle for most of us who work from home is that we feel guilty because we're at home and we can't manage to keep everything around the house done (because if we do that, we're not focusing on the business and bringing in money). If we focus only on the money, our personal standards of how we want our home to look and feel may suffer. And, yes, you can ask your family to pitch in. However, I do know that not everyone has a supportive family unit.

I sit down and use a day planner to write out my priorities for the day. It lists every client project that needs to be completed. I work off of two systems. I have a weekly master list and then I have a daily list. My day planner lists the day of the week and the date. It also lists times from 8 am to 6 pm. I don't worry about using the time slots. I just want the space to write my list. If you enjoy planning your work down to the time, go for it. While I try my best to start my work day by a certain time, it doesn't always happen. What's most important is to know what you need to do. I write down things in the order in which they should be done, from most important to least important (where possible).

Plan exactly what you want to do with your business. Start listing out goals. Your goals can be daily goals. They can be weekly goals. You can make monthly goals, quarterly goals, or yearly goals. You could do all of those.

After you've written out what you want to do as a business, you must assess the needs of your potential clients and you need to plan (yes, again) how you plan to reach out to your target market and how you plan to fill their needs.

So, why plan? You plan so that you can live by the 6P sentence: Proper planning prevents piss poor performance.

One of the reasons why people fail is because they don't take the time to plan. Planning doesn't mean everything is written in stone. It just means that you've taken the time to prepare yourself for the common occurrences associated with business. It is creating your road map.

Viability

When I first started writing for money, the first question I had to ask was: Is it possible to earn money by writing?

Most people that I knew said not unless you write a best seller. It never really dawned on them (or me at that time, anyway) that every single word you read on a website is written by someone. Every single word on a television show, in a movie, on an Amazon product description....all of it was written by someone. So, my first goal was to determine if it was viable.

Of course, I had to figure out my definition for viable. I was teaching college. I was working in a law firm. Would it be viable for me to replace one job or both jobs? Could I make enough money to replace those incomes?

When you're doing research, don't get sidetracked by people offering you "limited time" access to a course that will teach you how to make six-figures in your field overnight. There's no such thing as an overnight success. Instead, you're looking to find verifiable businesses who do what you do...or who do something similar if you're thinking way outside of the box. So, I looked for websites belonging to freelance writers. I looked for websites that offered freelance writing jobs of some kind (and I had to wade through some really crappy sites). I looked on social media and would check out the articles written by other writers. Those articles weren't about writing, mind you. I was looking for bylines so I could look people up to ascertain how often they published.

I'll talk about how to price your work later, but it must be touched on here because that's part of viability. You must know what you need to make in order to survive. This could mean that you have to pare down to the very basics of life (at least at first) in order to make the leap (something else I'll talk about later). The question to consider is from a realistic view, how long would it take for you to turn a profit and pull a paycheck to support yourself or your family?

Scheduling

The next plan you must make is how you will first start and work your business on the side of your current full-time job. Of course, if you've been unable to find work for a while, you can just jump headlong into the pool. For those who are working, take a long look at your current life. Take a long look at your responsibilities. Are you ready to give up what little free time you have to propel yourself to a better life? Are you ready to stay off social media after work and devote that time to your new business? Are you ready for late nights and early mornings?

Rule # 2 – Work Your Plan

Almost everyone that I know who started a business and failed knew the statistics about small business failure rates...and thought that they were magically going to overcome the odds. According to the Small Business Administration, only half of all businesses started will still be around in the next five years[1]. Depending on the industry, the failure rate during the first five years of business is as high as 95%. So, simply from the SBA, a government agency, we can summarize this as:

· You have a 50% chance of your business dying off within the first few years.

· Depending on the industry, your chance of survival is only 5%.

So, if the numbers are so bleak, why do people want to start a business? Wouldn't it just be safer to stick with traditional employment? Well, statistics are easily skewed (take the unemployment rate, for example. If a person remains unemployed for a certain length of time, they're just no longer counted as unemployed. They statistically stop existing so that the government can make themselves look good). Traditional employment is no guarantee of job security. I'm sure everyone remembers at least reading about The Great Depression and experiencing (or reading about) 2008. In 2008, while everyone seemed to be losing their homes, their jobs, and their retirement accounts, I was in the bankruptcy industry...and business was booming.

I've worked with a lot of people who wanted to start a business. Some have succeeded in at least creating a little extra income while others failed miserably. Why did they fail? Because they:

- Realized working from home was actually work

- They failed to work their plan

The existence of a plan for you to ditch corporate America and work from home doesn't do you a damn bit of good if you don't...work your plan.

It's all about commitment. You must be committed when things are new and exciting...and you must remain committed when things are a giant pain in the ass. There are days where you will want to quit. I know. I've worked from home for a while now and I still have those days. They're just part of life. You keep your head down and keep working. And that brings me to Rule 3.

Rule #3 – No Excuses

This rule never wins me any friends. First, you have to realize that pretty close to everything people say about why they can't accomplish something is an excuse. When you come home from your day job or when your children finally go to sleep at night after a day full of shenanigans, you're tired. I know you are. I worked full time and went to school full time and had a side business. I worked two jobs and started my freelance writing business. I know tired. Tired and I are best friends. If you don't work on your business because you're tired, that's an excuse. It may feel like a legitimate reason to you, but it's not. Every day that you ignore your business you reduce the likelihood that you'll be successful. Why? Because every day that you're stagnant it gets easier for you to remain that way. It gets easier for you to accept the status quo...and then you just start making other excuses. A body in motion stays in motion. Even if you're tired, you have to work on your business. Even if your children are sick, even if you are sick...doesn't matter. This is one of the most important rules because when you work from home, you do not get paid time off. If you're not working, you're not making money.

Business Plan Basics

Often, it is presumed that if you don't need financing to start your business, you don't need a business plan. To some degree, I guess that's true. Yet, a business plan isn't just about convincing someone else about how you plan to take the business world by storm. Instead, it's used to help you turn your dream into a reality. It's your road map. Business plans don't have to be complicated, especially if you don't need to show it to the bank or investors. You can make it as easy or as complicated as you'd like. You can make it formal or informal. In this section, I'm going to explain the different sections of a business plan and include some tips on how you can get through the business plan formation process without too much anxiety. And, yes, you can skip the business plan all together, but I've found that at least having an informal idea of what you want to do can help make it that much more real. It stops being just an idea – it becomes a feasible endeavor.

Before we get started, I want you to take a few minutes and shut your eyes. Specifically, I want you to visualize what life is like for you at the height of your business success. Write down your answers to the following questions…I'll explain why in a minute.

- What are you wearing?

- What does your office look like? Is it in a different building or do you have a home office?

- What about your home décor? Is it the same or have your changed some things?

- What would your ultimate day be like?

- Are you working alone or do you employ others?

- Tell me about your clients. What income range are they in? What do they do?

- What would your average meals look like in a day?

- How do you spend your free time?

- Tell me about how you interact with your clients. Are you on a first name basis? Do they go through an assistant to get to you?

- What colors would you use to describe your business? Would it be powerful and passionate colors like red? Would it be steadfast and soothing like blue?

- If I asked you to describe your new life with a song title, what would it be?

- If I asked you to describe your business with a song title, what would it be?

Yes, I know...some of the questions don't seem to make much sense...except they do. The answers to these questions will help do two things:

1. It will help you write a business plan that is geared toward fulfilling your future business goals.

2. It makes the idea of your business more real. Remember what you read earlier about visualization? It's true here, too. Visualization is powerful. It's almost like fake it until you make it. The more you see yourself doing certain things in your mind, the more you'll want to try it. This builds self-confidence. You'll begin to make what you visualized here into your own reality.

So, let's get started. I'll use my original answers to those questions. First, though, I want to tell you where I was and what I was doing when I answered these questions. It was fall 2009. Jacob was almost nine years old. Bryan was 11. For quite some time, Jacob expressed interest in playing football. For the most part, I was fine with it. I told him that he could play recreationally once he started sixth grade. Obviously, we were about three years away from that, but like most little boys, he loved tossing around a football. When I got in from work one evening, He showed me his index finger. It was swollen. I was angry. The school never called me. (When I talked to the school the following day, they said they didn't think it was a big deal). I hoped he jammed it. I took him for x-rays. They couldn't tell for sure if it was broken because of the swelling. We went to the doctor. Then, we got referred to a pediatric ortho specialist...just in case. They did more x-rays and found that his finger was, indeed, broken. The doctor recommended surgery so it would heal right and he could play football in the future.

The surgery was scheduled at a specialized orthopedic hospital. It was an outpatient procedure. I sat with Jacob while they gave him anesthetic. Then, I was sent out to the waiting room. And I sat...with a notebook. Yet, at the time, I wasn't thinking about writing as a profession. I wanted to find a way to use my Bachelor's in Paralegal Studies in my own business. And, yes, freelance (or independent) paralegals are really a thing. Even now. So, with nothing but time on my hands, I decided to kill time by writing down answers to those questions above. I ended up with a working business plan that I used. It worked. I used the same model when I started toying around with freelance writing when I taught Paralegal Studies courses.

Why do I tell you that story? Because I want you to recognize that you can start writing out a plan right now. It doesn't matter where you are. If you have your laptop, notebook, or even an online note system (like Google Keep), you can start planning. You can't get to your end result without a plan. Also, for those worried about it: NO, you do NOT have to start your plan as soon as you finish it. Sometimes when we plan, there's this pressure to instantly act. Yet, depending on your circumstances, you may need to take some other steps before you implement your plan. So, please understand that this isn't about anything more than just planning. Final note, you don't have to answer the questions in any particular order.

Business Goals

The very first thing I asked myself (and we will get to those other questions above) is: **what do I want to accomplish by starting a business?** Some of my answers included:

- More money to buy a house.

- Work with a variety of attorneys to get experience in several areas of law.

- Help consumers who can't afford the high cost of legal matters, such as Chapter 7 bankruptcy.

- Flexible schedule.

- Take real vacations.

- Make more money than I do now. <$30,000.

The next question I asked myself: **how do I define success?** Some of my answers included:

- Making at least $30,000 per year.

- Being home when my children needed me.

- Being requested by attorneys.

So, some of you may be scoffing at the $30,000 per year. I live in the Midwest. We have a very low cost of living compared to either the east or west coast. I made $25,000 a year as a bankruptcy paralegal. I didn't care as much about making more money as I did being able to support myself and my children. And, let's be realistic. It's much easier for us to think about starting a business when we think about money in terms of what we currently make. Sure, most people dream of big bucks. Money doesn't make you happy, but it goes a long way to making certain worries go away. If you've ever wondered how you'd pay your electric or water…or how you'd feed your family, you know what I'm talking about. That's one of the reasons why the direct sales marketing message of "What could you do with an extra $500 a month?" is so powerful. We all know which bills we could pay with it.

Yes, No, Hell No, Maybe

The next page in the notebook that I still have was divided into two columns. The column on the right of the page was horizontally divided into third. The column on the left was **"Yes."** Those were the things I could and would do. You'll probably laugh, but here's my first list:

- Chapter 7 bankruptcy

- Schmoozing

- Writing

- Brainstorming

- Editing

- Wills

- Objections

- Responses

- Problem Solving

- Can do attitude (Believe it or not, this is more important to business success than you'd think.)

- Meet deadlines

- Fast learner

- Research statute of limitations

- Write contracts that don't pertain to real estate

- Power of Attorney

- Scheduling

- Deposition summaries

- Background searches

- Finding social media profiles

- Skip tracing

- Business plans

- LLC documents

- Divorce forms

- Counter analysis

Notice how my list isn't necessarily a list of everything I can do. It's a list of things I wanted to or would do in business. At that time (remember, this was 2009), I was looking at things more like a jack of all trades. It took a while for me to refine my independent services. Just write down whatever comes to mind that you wouldn't want to make you drink bleach.

On the right side of my column I had my **"No"** column. The reason why it was a no wasn't because I didn't want to do it. It was because I knew I didn't have the knowledge or skill to do it. It had one single entry:

- Business taxes

Yeah, that's it. I felt like although I could form businesses, come up with plans, and help people come up with proactive solutions that I could not really help anyone with business taxes. It's really a fair assessment. I do my own taxes (although I have people I ask). I didn't want to get the necessary credentials or take the time to learn to do anyone's other than my own. I've taken several tax classes, but it's just not something I should do for others. I can give people basic info like you'll find in this book, but it's basic information from someone with experience and not an expert opinion. Taxes are so different from person to person, business to business. It's vital to speak with a professional.

Then, I had my **"Hell NO"** column. It was another one answer column:

- Receptionist

At that time, I was worn out of one specific task in my skillset: being on the phone. To this day, it isn't my favorite thing in the world. I probably won't ever love being on the phone, but when you own a business, you do what needs to be done. I'm very lucky in that most of my clients prefer email or private messaging.

Finally, I had my **"Maybe"** column. This column had something I was interested in that I didn't know much about:

- Marketing

So, what can you learn about my answers? I focused more on what I knew I could do while identifying a couple of areas I couldn't do and one that I would like to do, but didn't know enough about.

Now, we'll move onto the other areas of the business that will incorporate some of the above questions. Those questions are used to define the personality of your business. This is important because people (and other business owners) do business with people that they like. This information may seem unnecessary now, but in the long run, knowing this information can help you find the right audience. The right audience is important because you can't be successful without them. If you don't know your audience, you can't properly market your business to them. Let's get started with the main questions. You'll be able to see the other questions in my answers. I don't have a good reason for you as to why I asked myself these things. It just seemed to me (and still seems to me) that most businesses are an extension of the personality of their owners.

What's for Sale?

This really is the first thing you must ask yourself. People don't want to get involved in certain types of businesses because they seem more sales oriented than other forms of business. The thing is, all businesses are sales based. Even if you offer a service, you must engage in sales. You must convince others they need what you offer. You must sell your expertise. So, take some time and think about what your business and you have to offer. My answers included:

- Legal skills

- Convenience

- Delivery to home or office of legal forms and documents

- Motivation (more flexible, cheaper for consumers and solo lawyers), more experience for me, more control for me)

- Availability in a specific geographical area

- Personality (candid, upfront)

- Affordability

- Knowledgeable

Defining the Personality of the Business

To describe your business, you must be able to describe yourself. You must be able to figure out what sort of image or brand that you want your target market to see. Here's what I asked myself along with my answers:

- Songs (I picked two)

- Movies (I picked zero; I'm not into movies)

- Food – Italian, chili

- Drinks – Water, pure juice with no sugar

- Magazines – Focused on law; specifically, bankruptcy

- Travel – Warm places

- Interaction – Professional dress, firm handshakes, kindness, candid, approachable

- Colors and tastes – Rich, red, crisp, sapphire, smooth

- Clothing – Heels, skirts, blouses

- Meal – Mushroom stuffed ravioli with white sauce

- How I am different – Small business, creditor side bankruptcy experience, fewer bad habits because of less experience

What did you learn from my list about me? I'm sure if we met, you could practically guess how my business as a freelance writer is ran: straight, no nonsense, professional but easy to talk with (not to, but with).

Why Would Anyone Hire Me?

Next, I had to think about why anyone would want to hire me. That's not always a comfortable question to ask. So, if you have self-esteem issues, pretend that your very best friend wants to start a business and they asked you that question, but use your own answers. By the way, for this question, it's perfectly fine for you to use realistic answers. Here are my answers:

- Less overhead

- Lawyers: don't have to pay support staff for vacation, workers' comp

- Convenience; no need for consumers or lawyers to meet in person

Way back in 2009, I knew that remote work would be a big thing. One of the main reasons that individuals and business owners choose remote workers it to save on overhead and taxes. Think ahead. What do you see happening in the future?

Who Are My Customers?

You know as well as I do that if your business isn't making money, you've got an expensive hobby on your hands. You must know who your customers are. I looked at location, use, and what people would understand about what I offered:

- Location. I named various cities and towns to my area

- Use. Attorneys in need of a temporary paralegal; consumers needing help completing Chapter 7 bankruptcy forms or background checks

-   Customers would understand the savings they would get by contracting me on a per project or per hour basis. I also specific that no legal advice would be given (because it is illegal for paralegals to give legal advice)

Writing Your Mission Statement

Once you have the answers to the above, it's time to think about your mission statement. Writing a mission statement can overwhelm a lot of people. Here's what you need to know about writing a mission statement: it's not a "be all, end all" explanation of your business. You can change it later as your business changes. To write it, review your answers to the previous questions and choose the best words that would attract your target market. My first mission statement as an independent paralegal read:

Affordable administration by the project tailored to fit the needs of the client. Professional, knowledgeable, and convenience, clients have less overhead and more money. I'm not successful unless you're successful.

For the record, I didn't run around spouting this off as an elevator speech. Primarily, it guided me. Most of my clients learned about the contents of my mission statement by working with me.

Start-Up Costs

Next, I thought about start-up costs. What would I need to really get the business up and going (besides clients)? My list looked like this:

- Business cards: $25.00

- Website: $20 domain + monthly fee (At that time, I wasn't sure what the monthly hosting fee would be)

- Marketing: ? (It is perfectly fine to not have an answer and need to do some research.)

- Printer ink: $200

- Tax ID: $0 through IRS

- Receipts: $5 for a booklet (In 2009, cloud accounting wasn't common for small businesses.)

- Book keeping software: Have it.

- Getting set-up as an LLC: $100.

Then, I thought about things I would need to consider on a monthly basis:

- Getting an office would require monthly rent or I could work from home

- Cell phone

- Would I need to cover electricity with an office space?

- Would I need to collect sales tax for the city and state?

- How much money should I put back for Medicare tax, state tax, federal tax, etc?

My next consideration was capital expenses. Questions I considered:

- When will I need new software? How much will it cost?

- When will I need a new laptop or computer? How much will it cost?

- What sort of professional services (i.e., accountant, lawyer, marketer) do I need? How much will it cost?

- Are there any professional memberships I should pay for? Examples: Chamber of Commerce, CLEs, NALA, subscriptions, NALA certification, yearly renewal of LLC

You need an average, at least, of how much all of those items will cost you. You'll want to work them into the amount of money you'll need to make each year.

What about More Traditional Business Plans?

I know that there are many people who are reading this book and they're wondering whether they must use the simple business form templates that are provided above or if it's okay for them to use a more traditional business plan. The answer is yes, you can use a traditional business plan. Generally, the reason people tend to not use a traditional business plan when they are starting a freelance or work-from-home business model is it because it includes a lot of sections that simply may not apply to them. Also, from my experience, people tend to get frustrated with the more traditional business plan model.

In this section, we are going to look at the traditional sections of a business plan and go over some questions that you can ask yourself in order to complete this sort of plan. A traditional business plan generally has four sections. the first section is the executive summary. It is made up of several other subsections. The second section is the description of business. It is also made up of several subsections. The third section is the marketing section. It usually has four subsections. The last section of a traditional business plan is an appendix and it covers all of the information in more detail.

Executive Summary

The executive summary is a brief overview of your business. It covers the objectives of your business and any accomplishments. Generally, many people write the executive summary last although it is the first section of a traditional business plan. This is so that they can more easily summarize the information that is found in the plan. The first section of the executive summary is the highlights subsection. under highlights, you want to summarize key business information. You might highlight sales. You might show expenses. You might also give an overview of the net profit that you expect the business to make during the first few years.

Next in the executive summary area, you have the objectives of your business. You can even include a timeline of the goals that you want to achieve over the first few years at your business is up and running. If you do not have any traditional business experience, you might consider looking up business plan samples for businesses in your industry so that you can get a good idea of how objectives are worded.

Next, you will have your mission statement. You can also include any information about your business that won't be included anywhere else in the executive summary. Something you might consider doing is going to visit the website of your favorite retailer, small business, or vendor and looking at the way that their mission statement is worded. Of course, you can also refer to the information that you wrote down during the business planning process that we went through earlier in this text.

Some traditional business plans have one more subsection under the executive summary area of the business plan. That section is known as keys to success. In this section, you would explain distinguishing factors it's going to help your business succeed. This is really important particularly if your business is going to eventually need a loan or you plan to look for investors.

Description of Business

The next section is known as the description of business. You need to provide a clear and concise description of your business. Make sure that you rely on facts and not just ideas of what you think your business will become. However, you must also highlight what makes your business competitive and how those particular skills and talents will also make your business successful. the goal here is to highlight what will make your business attractive to your target market.

The first subsection under description of business is Company ownership. This is also known as legal entity. In short, this is the way that your business is structured under the law. For example, your business may be a sole proprietorship, a corporation, or a partnership. If you need licenses or permits to operate your business, you would include the requirements for getting those and where you are in the process of getting the license that you need to be in business.

The second subsection is location. Location can be extremely important depending on the type of business that you run. Of course, if you're working out of your home, you may not be so concerned about whether or not you have a storefront that's in a place where you're going to get a lot of foot traffic. However, that does not mean that you can Overlook the section. When you work from home, you must still ensure that you can operate that type of business from your home. One of the best things that you can do is simply find out how your home is zoned. Additionally, you can also check with the city commerce in your area or with city council. They should be able to tell you what sort of businesses can be ran out of the home.

The third subsection is interior. This could have evolved how much square footage you need to run the business, if you need to remodel any area of your house, or if you need to make any modifications to existing space. This section is particularly helpful if you plan to get funding.

The fourth subsection for description of business is the hours of operation. That's pretty self-explanatory, but it's still something that you should not skip just because you work from home. Also, keep in mind that because you work from home your schedule will likely change from time to time. So, you'll want to include information in this area that highlights the hours you will most likely be working.

The fifth subsection is titled Products and Services. You'll explain your products or services and why you believe that there's a demand for them. You'll want to discuss your target market and how what you're offering can be used to benefit them. You'll also want to highlight which products and services create a competitive edge.

If you provide products or certain types of services, you'll need a subsection to discuss how you plan to get the supplies that you need. This includes discussing billing information. For example, you pay Company A on a net 30 basis.

Next, all businesses using a traditional business plan model should have a subsection that explains the level of service that clients will receive before, during, and after the sale. I am a big believer in follow-up and properly building relationships with clients. Happy clients give referrals. Also, speaking of service, make sure that you and the client are on the same page for what you plan to do and what you are not doing. This can prevent a lot of misunderstandings and hurt feelings that could damage the ability to develop a long-term relationship.

The next section is manufacturing. You'll use it if you make products. If you do, what sort of special machinery, tools, or equipment do you need? Be careful not to reveal how you're making the product. This is not the place to explain proprietary information. Also, you'll want to explain how you plan to get your products to the public. Are you going to provide those products directly or will you use a distributor? If your products require shipping or some other form of transport, how will that be handled?

The next section applies to all businesses. Good ole' management. How does your background or experience help you successfully manage your business? Will you be an active manager or will you hire someone? Do you plan to delegate any areas of your business to the management to another person? If so, what are their qualifications and background? How do their areas of expertise help support the business? What responsibilities will they have? Are they a partner or just a manager? Will you need to hire additional people for management?

Moving onto the subsection of financial management, be glad that you're working from home. It's much easier, in my opinion, to keep costs low. Most home businesses don't need funding. There's a good chance that you're able to finance your own start-up costs. And that's really a good thing. Good financial management really is the difference between failure and success. Primarily, this section exists so that you can explain how your business will become and remain profitable. You'll also explain how long it will take for your business to become profitable. You should also consider the likelihood of past due accounts. Past due accounts affect your bottom line; and, if you ever were to seek out a business loan for any reason, the financial institution (or investor) will look at past due accounts as part of determining if you're a good risk. You will give a summary of the items in the appendix section: startup expenses, how much start-up capital you need, your cash flow, income projection, profit and loss statement, balance sheet, sales forecast, milestones, and a break-even analysis. You'll also want to create an operations budget. This will help you project expenses so that you can get a good picture of what it will really cost you to run your business. You should include your expenses (rent, utilities, insurance, payroll, taxes, loan payments, supplies, legal, accounting, marketing, maintenance, depreciation, and any other specific item that relates to running your business.

The final subsection is your start-up summary. You'll summarize key details about starting your business. If you don't feel that this section is necessary, you can eventually delete it. I do recommend that you include it while drafting your business plan. You may want to add some of that information to your executive summary.

Marketing

The next major section of a traditional business plan is marketing. Just because you work from home doesn't mean that you can forgo a marketing plan. Clients don't just fall out of the sky or hatch from an egg you found in a nest. No, you have to find clients and put yourself out there in front of them (over and over and over and over and over again). Marketing is an integral part of business success. (Yes, even on a freelance platform – your profile is a marketing tool!) You need to know who your market is, what they want, what they don't want, and what expectations they'll have of your business.

The first subsection is your market analysis. Who is most likely to need your services or products? What do you know about them? I'll explain more about determining your target market later in this book. You need to explain where you'll find your target market and how you'll show them what they have to offer. You should also consider whether the market you're trying to reach is growing, shrinking, or if it remains steady. What percentage of your target market do you think you can reach? Do you think you'll be able to increase your portion?

The second subsection is market segmentation. Are there different parts within your target market? That can affect what you offer and how it is offered. Which segment is your primary?

Next, you'll create a subsection for competition. Who else does what you do? Don't think about this in terms of your specific processes. Think about it on a broad level. Visit their websites. See how they conduct business. What are their strengths? What are their weaknesses? Find the percentage of the market that they reach. What can you do better? How will you compete? How will you stand out?

The next section is pricing. You'll need to explain your pricing policy and how you decided on your prices. You'll also want to address the pricing policies of your competitors. Are your prices similar to theirs? Are your prices similar to those charged within the industry? How will you keep an eye on profits and overhead to make sure that you're turning a profit?

Next, you'll address advertising and promotions. How do you plan to advertise your business? How will you decide how much to spend on advertising? How do you plan to track the results of your advertising? When will you advertise?

The next section is strategy and implementation. Summarize your marketing strategy and how you plan to implement it. As a new business, you'll want to prioritize the steps you need to take to get up and running.

Appendix

The appendix houses a detailed look at your start-up expenses, how you determined the start-up capital you'll need over a certain period of time, your cash flow over that same period of time, an income projection statement, a profit and loss statement, a balance sheet, a sales forecast, and any anticipated milestones you expect to hit. You can learn more about each of these by looking around online. It's important that you understand the elements to include in each document.

If you don't plan to use a traditional business plan, you should still understand how to construct each of these documents.

What If You Don't Want a Business Plan at All?

Uhh, well, okay. Just remember that a business plan is a road map that helps you create and run your business. It's not something set in stone. It's something you can change. It also doesn't have to be complicated.

If you **really** don't want a business plan, I still implore you to create a SWOT analysis. Don't worry – it's not as hard as a traditional business plan. It may, however, take you as long as my "not a business plan" method I talked about above. It is up to you how detailed you want to get with this. If you don't create any sort of business plan, I advise you to take ample time to consider the following and detail it out as much as possible because a SWOT analysis is all about creating a business strategy.

SWOT is an acronym. It stands for:

- **Strengths.** What are your strengths? What are the strengths of the business. Be realistic and be honest. Also, list things that your future clients would consider a strength of the business. If you really don't know, go do some research on other businesses in your industry. What do they offer? Do you offer similar things? Do you offer things that are different?
- **Weaknesses**. All businesses and people have weaknesses. It doesn't mean the business or the person is a failure. It just means that there are areas that need work. What won't your business offer? What aren't you capable of doing for your business

(such as taxes or payroll)? What could cause your business to lose a sale? What would potential clients not like about your organization? Again, be honest and realistic. The more you know about what you're going to do, the better off you'll be in the long run. Go back and re-read my rules above about planning to work and working the plan.

- **Opportunities**. Think about opportunities in multiple ways. How can you be of service to your target market? How can you solve certain problems? Are there certain business trends that present an opportunity to you? How can you get the word out about who you are and what you do? (Yes, I know "you hate sales!" Marketing yourself is a necessity. The stork does not drop clients out of the sky onto your door step.)
- **Threats**. What potential problems could hurt your business? Do others in your industry offer something you don't? Can you keep up with the changing space? Can you keep up with necessary technology? Do you have cash flow? Are you in debt up to your eyeballs? Revisit your weaknesses. Could any of those things fatally harm your business? Again, be honest. This is important stuff.

Once you have your SWOT analysis put together, you can better plan (oh, look, the rules again!) out your business and how it operates. You can also minimize potential disasters. There's another saying I use on a regular basis. It's known as the 6 Ps: Proper planning prevents piss poor performance. Let SWOT be your friend.

Rate Setting

There is more than one rate that you should consider. You need an hourly rate and you need a rate that you charge for various flat rate projects. Of course, if you plan to be a writer or editor, you need a per-word rate and you must take revisions or editing into consideration. So, think about what it is you want to do. Maybe even do a little research to see how others in your space charge.

In my experience, it's much easier to start with the hourly rate and then determine your flat rate. As you become experienced in business, you become assured of how long it takes you to perform certain tasks. You can use that amount of time and compare it to your hourly rate to come up with the right price. Usually, I make most of my money off of flat rate. If someone pays me $300 to write ten pages of web content, that comes out to about $30 per page. Most clients want around 500 words per page. They want it short and usable for their clients. I know it takes me around 30 minutes (or sometimes less) to write 500 words. So, two pages in an hour is $60 an hour. I usually charge between $37 and $45 an hour, depending on the project. Some projects, it takes me less time to write the content because I have substantial experience. So, I average as much as $150 an hour. It's a nice chunk of change. The crazy thing is that I know a few writers who charge $300 an hour. Ultimately, what you charge should be able to cover your expenses and make you happy with what you're making. What's the point of being self-employed if you can't take care of yourself and your family by breaking a glass ceiling or two?

So, how do you determine your hourly rate? Well, first you'll take the amount of money you need to make each year. Remember, you can base this number off of what you make now and what you need to survive. Then, you'll add your capital expenses, educational expenses, a tax estimate of around 25% and professional fees. Mine looked like this in the beginning:

$30,000 (salary)
+$800 (capital expenses)
+$500 (educational expenses)
+$400 (CLE / memberships)
+$7,500 (estimated taxes at 25%)
+$250 (professional fees)

$39,450 per year

Now, you may have noticed a couple of missing items: health insurance and business insurance.

You can add any expenses you want. You should definitely include taxes (although you can leave it out, but remember that you'll still have to pay your taxes; it's why I add mine in). I wanted you to see exactly what I started with because it's important for you to see that no business plan is perfect the first time it is written down. There's always room to change. Remember that I completed this very first plan while sitting in a hospital waiting room.

Now that you have what you need to make in a year, let's look at what you need to charge each hour. You must first think about how many hours you want to work in a week. I'm going to take you the "long" route because I know that there are lots of people who hate math (like me!).
1. Start by dividing your total by 12 because there are 12 months in every year. For me, that was $39,450 / 12 = $3,287.50. So, $3,287.50 each month.
2. Next, there are four weeks in every month. Take your total from step one and divide it by four. For me, that was $3,287.50 / 4 = $821.88 per week.
3. Now, how many days a week do you want to work? My children were in public school five days per week. My formula was: $821.88 / 5 = $164.38 per day.

4. Finally, how many hours each day will I work? I wanted to limit my hours to when the children were in school. They were gone from about 7:30 am until about 4 pm. So, I said eight hours (8 am to 4 pm – because I didn't care about taking a break at lunch. If you need a break, take it.). My formula was $164.38 / 8 = \$20.54$ an hour.

That's all it takes. I started freelance writing charging flat rate and charging around $10.00 an hour because I wanted to quickly gain experience. That worked for me, but I also had two other jobs (teaching college and working in a law office). I raise my rate now on a regular basis and I also take on a lot of flat rate work that makes me earn triple what I usually charge per hour. I also know I could continue to raise my rate and my client base (and the industries I serve) wouldn't bat an eye because the beauty of them choosing me over an employee is that they only have to use my services as needed…and there's less overhead for them.

Also, there's absolutely NOTHING wrong with starting at a lower hourly rate that's more than what you make. If you can keep yourself busy and make more money, do it. You can raise your rates as time goes on and filter out the lower paying clients as you take on the higher paying clients. That's exactly what I did.

Can You Really Run a Business from Home with Little Investment?

The answer to this question lies in what you want to do with your business. If you want to cater, have a bakery, or do something that requires you to deal with food or beverages, you'll probably have to invest more time and money to start up. In my state, it's practically impossible for people who want to sell their edibles to work (legally) out of their personal kitchen. You must have a food handler's license (which isn't a huge investment of time or money). You must have specific equipment in your kitchen or have access to a commercial kitchen. Of course, even if you have the commercial equipment in your kitchen, you'd need to have your kitchen inspected by the state on a regular basis. Oh, and you better check with your city or town hall about whether you can run a commercial enterprise of that nature from your home. If the answer is yes, you're going to want to them check with your landlord, if you rent, and your insurance company. Yes, you will need insurance.

I don't use the example of how difficult it can be to sell baked goods. I use it to show you that it's important to think about what you actually need to get started and to keep yourself out of trouble. To start a business, you must know what you need. Service-based businesses, such as writing and accounting, are the easiest to start. You don't need a lot of room. You probably have most of what you need. You probably don't need to find start-up capital. Easy peasy. Whereas, businesses that rely on physical goods (be it clothing, electronics, or kidneys...just kidding on the kidneys – that's illegal, don't do that!) create more issues. Not only do you need to think about start-up in terms of what you need to run your business on the administrative end, you also need money for your items. You may need extra room, too.

Be honest about what you need versus what you want. You may need a computer program or cloud-based app that has specific features. That's great. Do you really need the most expensive one on the market that likely does more than you know what to do with? Oh, and don't even think about pirating the software. You want people to pay you for your work. Those companies deserve the money for their work. They have programmers, developers, graphic designers, administrative staff, and sales staff to pay. They have costs associated with marketing, providing support, and the price to maintain servers.

One of the nice things about living in an age where there's a ton of choices is that we have more cost-effective solutions than ever before. Take your time. Find what works for you that falls within your price range. If it turns out that you really do need the most expensive software on the market and you can't afford it, find out whether you can get a license on a month by month basis. Adobe offers that option for many of their products. You would be able to access the software you need to make a profit. Then, you save money until you can afford to pay for a yearly or permanent license.

You should look for ways that you can save money. One way I do that is by not owning a printer. Yes, really. I'm a professional writer and I don't own a printer. Printer ink is expensive…crazy expensive, to use a technical term. My last printer was an all-in-one scanner, fax machine, and printer. The scanner was nice, but there's a smart phone app for that. Same with faxing. It was one of those machines that if you ran out of one color, you couldn't print anything…not even in black and white. Who needs that headache? So, anything I need to print gets placed on a flash drive. I take a five-minute drive to FedEx Kinko's and pay .08 cents a page. I keep my receipt and I write it off. It's much cheaper than buying printer ink and I think about whether I really need to print something before I do it.

When Should You Take the Leap?

I am a big believer in common sense. I am a big believer in doing whatever is necessary to take care of your family. I worked two jobs (taught college and worked in a law firm) while I built my business. There is a very good commonly held belief about taking the leap. You should have between three to six months of expenses tucked away before you take the leap. I did not abide by that rule. It is a good rule, though. However, I don't think someone should make the leap until they have built a good client base and they're losing money by turning people away.

One day, I sat in the law firm essentially doing nothing. Everything that I needed to do for the two lawyers I worked with was completed. I had several clients. Some were on the now defunct eLance. Some were on Odesk. Some were on People Per Hour. By the way, eLance and Odesk merged and created Upwork, where I now have approximately 50% or so of my clientele. I was getting up really early. I had already stopped teaching because I made more working with my clients than my teaching contract paid. Yet, I just didn't have enough time in the day. That day, I turned down several lucrative contracts because I didn't have the time to take on more clients. I sat there and did the math and realized that I was losing money by keeping the law firm job. My husband and I discussed it that night and I turned in my two-week notice. I had steady clients and a steady flow of potential clients. I could make $12.50 an hour at the law firm (just over $60 a day) or I could, at the very least, double that.

The moral of this section? Don't quit without a safety net of some kind in place. That could be three to six months of expenses (then you better be ready to burn the boat and make it happen) or it could be having clients in place and recognizing that you're literally losing money with your day job.

What about Incorporating?

This is probably one of the most common questions I'm asked: when should I incorporate? I'm not a lawyer. I don't play one on television, either. I can only speak from my personal experience as someone with a successful home business. First, don't hesitate to get legal advice about your situation. I know it seems like an expense, but it's really an investment into your business. It may even be considered a tax write-off. However, you'd also have to talk to a tax expert about that. I will never ever say that I am a tax expert, even with all the research I do.

When you first set-up shop, you're a sole proprietor unless you go through the steps to legally incorporate your business. There's nothing wrong with being a sole proprietor. Sole proprietorship is also known as "Doing Business As" or DBA. There are registered corporations that also have DBAs. You can still set-up a business bank account (always keep your business money separate from personal funds – and pay yourself from business funds). Outside of insurance that you may need for whatever it is that you do, sole proprietorship is the cheapest way to set-up a business. There's no paperwork that has to be filed at the state level for the creation of the business. Of course, you may still be required to get a sales tax permit or other permits.

If you've ever listened to Dave Ramsey (yes, the money guy), then you've probably heard his opinion on when to incorporate. You incorporate if you need to protect assets or yourself. Incorporation serves a very specific legal purpose (although different business entities have different benefits). They help shield the business owner from legal liability associated with the business. So, depending on which business entity you choose, you may not be liable on a personal level for business debts or if the business gets sued. If you're a sole proprietor and someone sues your business, or you have business debt, your personal assets are up for grabs.

There are lots of different entities to choose from: LLCs, C-corps, S-corps, partnerships, LLP, LP, and a few others. Whichever you choose will have a filing fee and it will also have a renewal fee. Depending on what you choose, you may also have to submit bylaws or other documents to the state. So, do your research and talk to a business lawyer to make sure that the entity you're interested in is right for you.

I have an LLC. It is considered a pass-through business. There's not much of a tax benefit outside of the fact that I can just use the Schedule C, my 1099 Misc (1099M) forms, and the usual 1040 to do taxes. I don't have a partner. I agree with Dave Ramsey: the only ship that won't float is a partnership. I don't want my business obligated because of the stupid decisions someone else makes. I don't want to be obligated, either. Also, the tax reform laws set in place by the Trump Administration has made having an LLC quite lucrative because a nice chunk of what I make is considered tax free. For my little business, it means I can hire other contractors. So, I'm able to help people learn the ropes of business and pay them to learn.

Scheduling

There's so much for me to say about scheduling. And I will, but first I will boil it down to one basic concept. You must control and protect your own schedule. If you're not working for one reason or another, you're not making money. If you're not making money, you can't pay your bills and keep your business afloat (especially in the beginning). Please, for your own success, protect your freaking schedule.

People are weird. You can spend all the time in the world building your business while you're working a traditional job. Some people will pat you on the back. Some people will call you a workaholic. Some people will applaud you for living the dream. Some people will tell you that you're wasting your time. Now, here's the crazy part. Say you get to the point where you start working from home full time. By the way, what I am about to say happens regardless of whether you have your own children or other reasons why you want to work from home besides "It looks cool and I hate my boss."

When you start working from home, everyone (and I mean everyone regardless of whichever comment they made from the last paragraph will have the assumption that you have free time and that you should run their errands or babysit their children because they "have to work" and you're at home anyway.

So, let's look at what's wrong with that scenario besides the obvious insult to those of us who work from home. I mean, because it's clear they've never ran a business or even worked from home with a traditional employer. Let's say you run their errands during the day. You're gone all morning. Hell, maybe you're gone all day. You also have your own personal or family responsibilities. You also must eat at some point. You get home and you're tired. That client work you should have done today doesn't get done or you stay up all night and work. Babysitting someone's children? That's going to include multiple interruptions and probably nerve-wrecking guilt because you're working. Of course, you're going to deal with the interruptions if you have children of your own. Being responsible for someone else's children on top of your own responsibilities creates even more stress for you.

See, there's this general idea among those who don't work from home and even people who are new to working from home that they can work whenever they want. It's an idea that attracts many people to the work from home lifestyle. It's technically true, but it can create big problems for you and for your clients.

1. **The time that you're not working is time that you're not making money.** You cannot rely on the "do it later" mentality. Procrastination is betting on the fact that future you isn't as tired, lazy, or busy as current you.
2. **Later may never come.** Yes, really. You're tired. You've got family or personal responsibilities. You get sucked into the latest TV show. Whatever. You don't get around to it. You miss a deadline. You lose a client.
3. **You rush through your work to try to make the deadline.** Gee, how could this possibly go wrong? I'm here to tell you that many projects take longer than you think. Rushing through could mean that you don't give the client your best possible work. It could mean you miss something crucial. It could mean that you screw up your reputation. All because someone wanted you to take care of X because they "have to work." Because, you know, they don't think what you do is valid enough to warrant your full attention.

4. **You miss the deadline because you didn't have enough time to work.** How happy do you think your client will be? Guess what? Your friend or family member who wanted you to do X for them isn't going to pay you what the client would have. They'll likely treat you like it's your fault or tell you that no one can really work from home and be successful.
5. **You stay up at night to work.** This leads to burnout unless you're a night person. Even if you're a night person, you're not going to get enough down time if you're doing crap for other people all day.

A second important consideration related to your schedule is your own natural energy level. When do you naturally feel the most energetic? Would it be reasonable for you to work during that time given your personal demands and your client needs? This is important because if you're doing something that's going to require a lot of client contact, making calls on behalf of the client, or they want you to be available during certain hours, that's something that must be considered. It's one of many, many reasons I don't work as a virtual assistant. There's absolutely nothing wrong with being a VA. In fact, I regularly help people find VA work. However, a lot of the time, the VA is expected to be available during certain hours. And if you get a client who is in a different time zone than you? Well, that can make your life difficult if the time you need to be available for the client is during a time when you'd rather be sleeping or spending time with family.

Speaking of scheduling, you need to truly consider how many clients you hope to have or how many it will take to support your lifestyle. The ideal scenario is that you can work on client projects all during the same timeframe. You could be in for one hell of a time if you have five clients and all of them need you at different times of the day or night.

So, when you're talking to clients, make sure that you get and stay on the same page when it comes to availability.

Whatever schedule you set, make sure that you stick to it. Pick the days and hours that will primarily work for you. I know that there are school field trips, the occasional lunch out, and that coveted afternoon nap. It's cool. I get it. If you know in advance that something is coming up, use your Out of Office reminder (OOO reminder) in your email of choice. It should say that you're attending to other matters (it's really not anyone's business what you're doing) and that you'll respond to emails and return any messages as soon as you reasonably can. And then do just that.

If you think that you're going to offer consultations, find and use the right calendar tool. Google Calendar allows you to set-up appointments (or so I've been told – I don't use it). There are also free apps and paid apps that you can set-up. People would visit your website (or a website address that is assigned to you by the provider) and enter in their details for the time and day of their choice. You'd get an email or some sort of notification letting you know that you have a consultation that's been scheduled. There are some that even allow you to collect payments. You may find that helpful in the future to protect your time and deter "tire-kickers" who aren't doing more than looking to get as much free information out of you as they can. Of course, I'm all about giving free advice that's actually helpful (maybe not in extreme detail – I have paying clients who need my attention). The purpose of giving out that advice is to show that you know what you're talking about.

Something else I can't say enough (but I'll spare you and just say it once)...for the love of cheese make sure that you actually USE your calendar. I don't care if it's Google Calendar, Apple, Yahoo, a paper planner...draw on your walls – whatever. Just stay on top of your calendar for deadlines. Give yourself ample time to work on projects.

My motto is under-promise and overdeliver. I'm a pretty fast worker, especially when I'm focused. Probably helps that I love what I do. Even when I didn't love my job, I was generally faster than all of my coworkers and that always caused a problem for me in the office...but I digress. If you think it will take a week to research and write a 10,000 word ebook, agree to a two week deadline. It's fine if you turn it in early, but what you do NOT want to do is turn it in late or figure out that life happens and suddenly you're not as on top of your stuff as you should be. So, please, use your calendar and use it wisely.

While you're at it, I want you to find three hours somewhere during your work week and schedule time for you. I don't care if it's to take a hot bath while the kids are at school, get a manicure, or go out and play in the dirt (garden). Do SOMETHING for you. Try to spread it out over the week. Mark it on your calendar. This is, barring an actual emergency such as your house burning down around you, non-negotiable. You need that time to feel human. It's very easy when you work from home to end up working all of the time in some capacity. If you're not working on client projects, you're doing something around the house that was neglected. I don't care how introverted you are (I can barely be measured on personality tests because of how introverted I am). You need that time. You are not a machine. So, schedule that time. Take that nap. Go out to lunch. Whatever. I have so many hobbies I can't even keep track. I just pick one and do.

Understanding Your Target Market

You are now entering one of the most important chapters of the book. This is the chapter that affects everything from how you market to how you interact with your clients...and even what your clients will pay you for your services. You must understand your target market. Full stop.

I know...I know...some of you are already freaking out, "Oh my God, but Robin, I don't know who my target market is! I just want to not have to go to the 9 to 5 and deal with traffic and pay for daycare and worry about sick leave or using my vacation because little Johnny has a stomach bug every two weeks like clockwork!"

So, take a deep breath before you do anything else. Do not skip this section. You need this section. We're going to do a little exercise together. You do not and should not rush through this section. Spend time answering the questions. Dream big. Yes, it's okay to dream big. It is equally okay to just want to make enough money to get by. Don't feel bad about whether you want to make a lot of money or just be financially comfortable while working from your couch. My goal was to just replace my income (and make a little more so that I didn't feel so stressed out by bills). Then, things got better. As I got more comfortable, I started changing up my game plan because I had more confidence in what I was doing.

Let's talk about your ideal client. Let's start with some basics: demographics. Yes, really. What do you imagine they do for a living? How much do they make? What is their life like? Where do they live? Where they live is important because cost of living often affects what people are willing to pay for certain things. What sort of clients do they have? How do they talk? Are they friendly or all business? Do they work in a fast paced industry or are they more relaxed?

Yeah, I know. I'm asking you to answer a lot of questions about someone you've never met. That's why I told you to dream big. In your ideal scenario, what would your answers be to those questions? Take a few minutes and write them down. Don't just think them out. Write them down. I don't want you to forget them.

This information is like gold. It can help you set your pricing. A mom and pop shop who needs a copywriter may not be able to afford someone who charges $400 an hour (even for a one- or two-hour copy job). However, it's likely they can afford $75 an hour or $100 an hour especially when they recognize that they're getting just as good, if not better, service than someone charging four times as much. You'll recognize who you can charge more. No, I'm not suggesting price gouging. I work primarily with professional industries (think copy for lawyers and writing textbooks). I still charge under what I could actually charge. Why? Because I like referrals. I like repeat business. I like being the first person people think of when they need copy or they find out their colleagues need copy.

Maybe you can't get in front of your ideal client just yet because your ideal client expects someone with a certain level of experience. However, creating and maintaining a profile will help you in the future with your proposals and your marketing.

You can, by the way, create more than one ideal client profile. You can create a profile sheet for anyone in any industry that you're interested in working with. Oh, and no one ever told me to do this. I wish I would have known to do this because it would have helped me so much with my business in its beginning stages. I used to feel really bad about charging between $12 and $20 an hour for work. I also had no idea on how to go about marketing myself. I knew I shouldn't use just one standard copy and paste proposal or cover letter. That's about all I knew, though. I had no idea on where to find clients. I actually didn't come across this concept until around 2016. I went through the process and refined my marketing from there. About a year after that, I was routinely working with companies (and individuals) who more closely fit my ideal client persona.

Oh, and this isn't just about marketing (although knowing where to find your target market is pretty freakin' important). It's also about making sure that as you get experience, you're often working with people you like and who respect what you do (I will not work with assholes no matter what they offer me in pay. I've even been known to fire clients after they show their true colors…). You'll also work on projects you like versus taking what you can to gain experience, get paid, and make a name for yourself.

My final tip for this section is to use this same process when you're trying to figure out who you should enter into a mentor relationship with. Sometimes this is easier if you think about what you want out of the future. If you had a perfect life (or at least as close to perfect as life could get you, what would you want out of it? Where would you live? What sort of clients would you have? How much would you make? Find someone who already embodies those things (or as close to those things as you can get; many people don't walk around blabbing about what they make).

Proposals

Proposals. It's a word that makes many people cringe. Know this: when you're starting a business of any kind, you must learn how to sell. I know, I know...you don't like smarmy selling. Selling makes you uncomfortable. Well, unfortunately there is not a stork who will magically drop clients off on your door step. There is no fairy who turns packages of ramen into living, breathing clients who want to shower you in cash.

You must be able to sell yourself as well as what you do. Why should your potential client choose you over the dozen plus other individuals and agencies who want to help them? What in the hell makes you so great? And, seriously, don't be shy about this. Be personable. Be likeable. Use proper language, but don't be too stiff. Understand what it is that your target market wants (which I'll talk more about in marketing).

So, after Upwork featured me in 2017, I got a lot of friend requests on social media. And lots of new freelancers and struggling freelancers asking for my help. I spent about a week reviewing profiles and making suggestions. Even if you aren't on Upwork or any freelance website, you'll still find value in these tips:

Just because you're in business doesn't mean that people will just throw money at you. You must make yourself (and your proposal) look and sound good. If you were in your clients shoes and had a dozen options or more to choose from, are you going to go with the proposal that looks copied and pasted and that ignored your needs? Are you going to choose the one with the typos? Of course not. You're going to choose the one that impressed you...the one that addressed your requirements.

There is no shortcut. Creating and sustaining a business is work. There's no magic pill. Unless you're blackmailing a billionaire, you're probably not going to wake up tomorrow with millions or even a few hundred thousand in the bank. Again, there is no shortcut. You have to work just like those of us that successfully run a business worked and continue to work. There's this thought that businesses "automated." That doesn't mean what you think it does. Unless you're Stephen King or another author getting a big fat royalty check each month, automation and "passive income" will mean how well your business works (such as through a chatbot) and what you've invested into your retirement account for the future. Buying into a business opportunity or even buying an actual business from another person is absolutely no guarantee of success. Especially if you start screwing with a proven formula because you think that, without experience, you can somehow do it better.

Even if a shortcut existed, it should be ignored. Why? Because if you're willing to take a shortcut on what could be the best and most profitable experience of your life, you'll probably take shortcuts on client projects, think you know more than your client does (and maybe you do, but it is ultimately their project), won't take direction, and you'll get upset when your client no longer wants to use you.

No one owes you anything. There isn't a single platform or person in existence that owes you anything. Yes, I know you didn't choose to be born, but you're here. Your life is what you make of it. Upwork or Fiverr or any other freelance platform doesn't you crap. Neither does Facebook, Twitter, LinkedIn, or Instagram. Your target market doesn't even have to give you the time of day. You earn your keep. And I promise you that it is better this way because you respect the process, the pain, and you enjoy the pleasure of the lifestyle far more.

Take advantage of the advice offered to you by professionals. You're reading this book for a reason. I was featured by Upwork for a reason. I remain a sought-after copywriter who works from home for a reason. I know what I'm talking about. You can't decide to change a proven formula and then bitch that you didn't get the results you wanted. When people in your space who have experience offer you advice, take it and say thank you. It's certainly up to you whether you follow it or not.

So, now that I have that out of the way, let's talk about writing a good proposal, shall we? Proposal writing is an art. When I first started, I probably had five or six basic proposals. They all said practically the same thing except I'd change up certain phrases or move things around. I'd use various ones in various industries (and edit the proposal to be specific to the job) and see which version worked better. This is known as A/B testing or split testing. It is your friend. Let's get started:

Screen potential clients. Yes, really. I know you're wanting to get as many clients as possible so you get money rolling in. Before I tell you what I do to screen potential clients, let me tell you what I am NOT doing. I am NOT necessarily basing my decision to work with someone (or not) based on whether they're new to business or new to whatever platform they met me on. For Upwork, I'll work with new people on the platform even if they don't have any feedback...if we have a nice, long discussion first and I am able to verify who they are...and that they have a verified payment method. That's important. I need to make sure I get paid just like you need to make sure that you get paid. For all potential clients, I look at:

A. The details of the job (I'll explain more on that soon).

B. If there's a deadline. If so, I need to determine if I can meet it. Deadlines are important.

C. The client's overall feedback score if I met them on a platform.

D. The feedback left for the client on the platform. I'm looking to determine if the client is unresponsive or otherwise seems to be a pain in the ass. I won't work with anyone who strikes me as being a pain in the ass.

E. If there is a preferred location or time zone.

F. The average rate the client paid in the past. This isn't always a deal breaker, but it can tell me if they're likely to consider my proposal or if they're going to likely hire someone in an area where the cost of living is much lower.

G. The number of applicants to the job if it is posted on a platform. If there is just one opening and it has 75+ applicants, I'm probably not going to waste my time unless I really, really want to work on that project.

H. The date the client last reviewed the job on the platform. If the last time the client bothered with the posting was two weeks ago, they've changed their priorities. This is a big red flag for me because what stops them from dropping off the face of the earth during the time I'm working on their project? Responsiveness is everything.

I. For platforms, I look at how many people were invited to apply and how many people are actively involved in the interview process. If two people were invited and one or two are interviewing, it's likely that the job was really created just for those people. I'm not going to waste my time.

Review the details of the job. Do NOT write your proposal until you read the job description (and understand the requirements). You will refer to the job details when you write your proposal. Read it carefully. Read it more than once. Make sure that it lines up with what you expect out of the project and with the budget. It's not always going to match up with a stated budget (if there's even a stated budget). Sometimes, the potential client won't know what sort of budget to set. They might set something really low and not address it in the job description. This doesn't need to necessarily deter you. However, if they say they want an "expert" and the job description says they're only going to pay you $2 an hour, that's a problem. However, let's say the budget is good. Look for keywords and phrases used by the client that you can address in your proposal. Also, if you're on a freelancing platform, look for required phrases. The client may want you to type "blue velvet monkey" at the top of your proposal as proof you read the entire job description. Don't leave out anything like that. I know it's silly, but it makes clients feel better.

While you're reading the job description, come up with at least one question to ask. Even if you think you understand everything perfectly, figure out something to ask. Yes, even if you know the answer. The question(s) you ask are an integral part of constructing a great proposal. Think about exactly how you can help the client. How can your experience or knowledge directly benefit the client IF they choose you?

The proposal writing process. Alright. Let's talk about the good stuff. A great proposal is NOT copied and pasted. Yes, it's okay to have one or two (or five) basic proposals you can pull from. However, if you're not customizing your proposal to the job, the client will know and they will probably ignore you.

Being invited to apply to something is a bit different than writing a standard proposal. When I'm invited, I am a little more direct because they already know who I am:

A. Hello FIRST NAME

B. I thank them for inviting me to bid on their project.

C. I tell them that I'm excited to learn more about their project and their needs.

D. If I have actual questions, I ask them. This could be something as basic as "Could you tell me a little more about the results you're looking to achieve?"

E. I ask if there is a deadline.

F. I mention something from the job description that can connect us. For example, if a lawyer asks me to bid on web content, I tell them approximately how many other lawyers in that area of law I've helped and the types of content developed (i.e., landing page).

G. I'll talk about previous experience and similar jobs, but from the perspective of how it can help them. This is not a "Robin is so great" section. It is me translating how they can directly benefit from what I do.

H. I always tell them that I look forward to hearing from the soon.

I. I use a professional sign off. "Best, Robin."

When I am not invited, my process is a bit different:

A. Professional greeting. I usually use "Good morning" or "Good afternoon."

B. Brief introduction that also includes my desire to know more about their project. "My name is Robin Bull. I'm a top-rated full-time writer and editor here on Upwork. I'd love to know more about your project." For referrals from existing clients, I just introduce myself as I would if they were a new connect. "My name is Robin Bull. I help CLIENT with X. CLIENT said that you were struggling with X. Is there anything I can do to help?"

C. I ask questions. Standard questions for me include: How often do you need blog posts? Do you provide keywords or topics? On average, how many words per post? Do you have specific days in mind you'd like to receive content?

D. I explain why I'm asking questions if I ask more than one or two. "I ask a lot of questions because I want to make sure that you get exactly what you want." See how I made it about them? ("...you get exactly what you want.")

E. Sometimes, I'll go into my education and experience if and only if it makes sense. This can be a bit long so I'll spare you.

F. I close with how I look forward to hearing from them.

So, let's talk about what I didn't do:

I did not go out of my way to overwhelm the client with information. Broken down like above, it may seem like I did. When I drop names or provide my experience, there's a reason for it. It is okay to cherry pick. You only need to include information that is relevant.

I did not beg for the job or ask for it. You can ask for it if you want, I guess. I basically said, "Hey, I'd like your consideration. Here's some questions…" I want to give them relevant information that benefits them. I told them I looked forward to hearing from them. Do not bombard the client with demands to hire you or beg them to hire you. Desperation won't get you hired by a good client. It might make you a sitting duck for someone looking to take advantage of you.

I did not copy and paste something. I followed a formula. I read the job description. I replied accordingly.

So, why is it important to ask at least one question? Well, I want to give the client a reason to respond. Most people will not ignore a genuine or well-posed question about their project. People LOVE to talk about their needs. The question is how I engage them. Even if they have their eye on another candidate, they'll remember me in the future.

What should you do if you don't know what price to bid? In addition to looking at any previous history if you're on a job platform, you can also just do a little market research using the Internet. What is the average price for the service? Given your experience and your needs, adjust the price. Yep, it really can be that simple. Oh, and trying to undercut everyone will eventually be bad for business for you. You'll end up with a schedule full of people paying below market prices. You'll make less than you need and you will quickly grow jaded with the whole process. Don't do that to yourself.

You can follow up with potential clients, but don't make a nuisance out of yourself. Wait a few days after you've sent your proposal before you try to contact them about it. Be kind and professional. And keep it short. If you're emailing, make sure you ask if there is anything else they need from you. Questions provide room for engagement. Do not beg. Do not annoy.

No Experience? No Problem!

A large portion of my readers are thinking the above is all well and good for someone who has experience, but what about people without experience? I am so glad you asked.

Everyone has to start somewhere. It can be hard to get the first job or two under your proverbial belt. Those jobs also need to go really, really well so that you get recurring work, referrals, or great feedback on a freelance platform. When I first started on Upwork, it wasn't even called Upwork. It was called oDesk. I was teaching paralegal courses for a local technical college. I had no publishing credits. I started a HubPages account and started creating various forms of content. I did my best to make my writing as professional as possible to show off what I was capable of creating. I wrote a few evergreen blog posts. I used both my HubPages content and my own content as samples.

As I started to land work, I'd make note of where the blogs or articles were posted. Provide that I wasn't under an NDA, I would share the links when asked for samples. I also created a few sample articles on basic legal concepts. I converted them to PDF and stored them in DropBox. I created share links for those. I also made it a point to keep my portfolio on Upwork up-to-date. I also updated LinkedIn quite a bit. I don't really update the Upwork profile much now...although I probably should. Who doesn't prefer more recent content? I have over 2,000 hours logged and a ton of feedback. So, potential clients now have a way to learn about who I am and what I do.

You can easily create a free portfolio by setting up a Wix site or even a WordPress blog.

Marketing

One area where practically everyone gets stuck is marketing. People, from my experience, fall into two camps (unless they already have professional marketing experience):

Those who don't market at all for one reason or another.

Those who try to do everything all at once.

Some of the main reasons why people don't market at all include:

Thinking that starting a business means people will bang down their door. I have bad news for you. There is no such thing as a client fairy. No one ever left a client on my door step or threw one at me in the beginning. I'm writing this book approximately five years into working as a full-time writer and content strategist. It's only been the last couple of years that I've had an onslaught of referral work.

They're afraid of it. Think about it – we're subjected to advertising practically all the time. We get stuck with imposter syndrome. You know, thinking you have no business doing what you're doing although you know on some level you have just as much (if not more) talent and skill as others in your chosen industry. They don't know what to say. They don't know what to do.

They don't think they have a budget for it. Yes, marketing can be expensive. However, there are some free and practically free things you can do to get and keep your name out there.

Then, you have people who throw money into practically every single freakin' way to advertise that they can think up. They generally get no results. Or not enough to justify the cost. They get frustrated and quit. They shut down their business. Why does this happen? Well, the bold truth of the matter is that they didn't take the time to do the research on:

Which advertising methods would work best to reach their target market;

What sorts of advertisements work best to talk to their target market; and

How to properly use the marketing channels they're interested in.

Oh, and then we have the new business owners that get sucked in by some fast-talking "online marketing expert." I'm talking about the ones that use jargon and never really give a clear answer to a question…or make it too intimidating to ask a question. People don't want to feel stupid, so they just blindly assume that this individual knows best. Sadly, the "expert" may not even have experience helping business owners in certain industries. This is important because certain industries have certain rules that must be followed. Take the legal industry as an example. I work with a lot of lawyers. From the time I took a legal ethics to paralegal class almost ten years ago to now, I've had it pounded into my skull that there are certain rules lawyers must follow when it comes to their advertising. They must supervise anyone they outsource their marketing to so that they can ensure that no ethical rules are broken. There are also federal laws (and sometimes state laws) that must be followed, depending on the industry. Take herbal supplements as an example. There are laws on the books that state these companies (and products) may not guarantee or claim certain results unless they can prove that their products work in certain types of testing. Not their own testing, either. And lots and lots of these companies come up with "studies" to "suggest" that their formula is absolutely amazing.

So, if you choose to hire someone to work with, do some research first to understand your target industry, where to find them, and what you believe may work best.

Free and Next to Free Marketing

Anyone who knows me also knows that I love a good bargain. I'm also all about some DIY. Then again, I love to read. I love to try to implement processes. Even if I'm not very good at doing something in the end, I love knowing the basics of how something works.

While it's important to set a marketing budget, I know that it's likely that you're investing money from your day job or maybe you don't have anything to invest at all. I get it.

There are some free and next to free marketing things you can do. The thing is, though, you must be willing to do it. And you must be consistent. There is no such thing as one and done when you're in business. Think about big businesses in your chosen industry. They probably have an entire marketing department and a social media department...even if they could probably coast on brand recognition for the rest of their lives. While the term "brand" gets thrown around a lot right now, that's exactly what you're doing: building a brand. When you're self-employed, your entire being is the brand...from the marketing material that goes out to how you behave on social media (even your personal accounts).

First, make sure that you have social media accounts set-up wherever you think that you may find your client base. No, you do not have to set-up business pages. What do I mean by that? Take Pinterest and Instagram as examples. If you have a personal account, you'll have an option under settings to switch to a business account. I haven't bothered doing that. Instagram is owned by Facebook. It's a well-known fact that the more fans / likes you have on

Facebook, the more they limit your reach particularly if people aren't liking or commenting on your posts. Why do they do that? Because they want you to pay them. No, I am not opposed to paying. However, if you don't know anything about Facebook marketing and their ads, it can be hard to get a good return.

So, start a Twitter account if you don't have one. Start a Facebook fan page. My accounts on Twitter and Facebook share the same extension: therobinbull. Start an Instagram just to get your name out there. Again, I use the same name: therobinbull. The nice thing about Instagram is that I can feed my images straight to my personal Facebook profile. I can also feed them to Twitter.

Twitter and Instagram

Twitter and Instagram have something in common. They both rely on hashtags. The more interaction you can get on a hashtag, the closer you move to the top...you know, what the cool kids call "going viral." How you'll choose hashtags will ultimately be up to you. There are websites devoted to hashtags. Find them. Read them. Learn them. I don't care if you don't like them. I'm not necessarily a huge fan. I stick to ones I believe would be relevant to my readership or to my potential client base.

You can get followers in several ways. Don't buy them, by the way. Every so often the social media gods go through and remove fake followers. One of the most popular methods is the follow back. You find several people or businesses you like. You follow them. If you're lucky, they follow you back. You can look at their follower list and who they follow. You may be able to find some good potential followers by repeating the same behavior.

With Instagram, there's a method I use called the 3, 2, 1 method. I learned this from Natalie Diver Ellis' YouTube channel. Find an account that you think belongs to someone who would find your posts valuable. Like three of their photos, leave two comments (not asking them to follow you – use legitimate comments...these are real people!), and follow them.

I don't use my Instagram to really seek out clients. I write for a living. Primarily, I use it to share my life and some of my work. I want people like you to see that normal (well, that's probably pushing it) people like me successfully work from home. It helps encourage people to do it.

Facebook

When you start a Facebook page, make sure that you fill out its profile completely. Use a cover image. Upload a profile photo. Then, invite everyone on your list of friends to like it. Don't prejudge others. If they like it, great. If they don't, whatever. In the beginning, it's downright silly (in my opinion) to sponsor posts or pay for a Facebook ad (unless you know what you're doing).

One thing I've learned from using a Facebook fan page is to share a lot of images. I'm a dry witted work from home wife and mom. I have a fairly dark sense of humor. I share all kinds of images that I know will get some sort of interaction. I also share every single image or link (with a description) to my personal page. This helps increase reach. When others like your post or comment, that increases reach. So, when you post images, don't be afraid to ask a question or to write something as an update at the same time.

If you have a blog (start one, by the way. It's as cheap as free or as expensive as you want to make it, but I'll talk about that in a minute!), connect it to your Facebook fan page so it will auto-feed when you publish something on it.

These little steps may seem like nothing, but they help you in the long run.

Hashtags work on Facebook, but not as well as on Twitter and Instagram. You can tag other Facebook pages. Sometimes, depending on how you upload and access your fan page, you can tag images with your friends from your personal profile. However, don't spam people. If you make a nuisance of yourself, people will unfriend you.

Oh, and just a head's up: if you currently spend your time pimping out your business on your personal Facebook profile, you could get into a lot of trouble by the Facebook police. They may suspend your profile or delete it altogether.

If you begin exploring Facebook ads, I have one piece of advice for you. However, first I must give a disclaimer. I hardly ever sponsor my posts. I also do not create ad campaigns for anything I do as a writer or strategist. I've done it for others. Facebook often changes their rules related to what they'll let people sponsor or promote through an ad campaign. They run a good game telling you about the potential reach you'll get, but if you don't understand how to use their tools to properly target your ad, you're probably just wasting your money. So, before you sink your time, your sanity, your any money into Facebook ads or sponsored post, watch videos on YouTube (recently published) about the process. Read articles by reputable marketing companies. Specifically research "how to target the right audience with Facebook ads."

There's absolutely no reason to spend a load of money on someone's course on how to create great Facebook ads unless you truly have an interest in it (or unless you're looking to possibly have a write-off for your taxes).

Yes, You Need a Blog

I don't care what industry you're breaking into. You need a blog. As I said earlier, you can make this as cheap or as expensive as you want. You can use WordPress (my personal favorite), Tumblr, or Blogger to start with a free blog. Please, for the love of all things work-from-home-holy, choose an appropriate name that reflects you as a professional or your business. Try to make it something that is easy to spell and easy to remember. I have several sites. I have two free Wix sites. One is a really old one. It's the one I first started my portfolio on. I keep it around to show people just how fast and easy it can be to get an online presence set-up. I created it before I had any real understanding of SEO (and that is not something you need to really worry about in the beginning; you can work on perfecting your presence as time goes on).

I've tried both Blogger and WordPress. I also have a Tumblr (or two) that I rarely use. I prefer WordPress. There are a lot of free themes that you can choose from and it's easy to use. You don't have to buy a domain. If you want to do so and you don't have any experience using CPanel to deploy WordPress, do yourself a favor and just buy your domain through WordPress. It'll cost you around $40 for the entire year.

So, the real questions about blogs:

1. How often should you update it?
2. What should you write about? This question will be answered in the next section.
3. Can anyone monetize a blog?

As far as how often you should update your blog, best practices change on a regular basis. I'll tell you the same thing I tell me clients. I don't care if you decide to update once a week or seven times a week. Pick something and stick to it. Seriously. The Google gods prefer websites that are updated on a regular basis. And, please, no keyword stuffing. You don't need to try and use your SEO keyword (because I'm sure you're already considering what words to use) in every paragraph. If you don't know anything about SEO, it's fine. Just start updating. You can look at what others in your space are doing. You can also read articles on content marketing. You'll probably feel lost at first, but eventually you'll get a good understanding of how often you should update and other best practices. I highly recommend Search Engine Journal. It's a free website. Also, many of their sister sites are also fantastic resources.

For the answer to the second question, move on down to the next section. The short answer is: write about things your target market wants to know about.

Monetization is a hot topic. There are courses, blogs, websites, "turnkey systems," and pins (on Pinterest) that promise to teach you how to make a gazillion dollars in 30 seconds of your spare time with blogging. Do not fall for the hype. Here's the rundown on monetizing:

- **Any company that might contact you or that you might approach to pay you for a sponsored post will want to know your metrics**. This includes your standing in the search engines, how many subscribers you have, how many visits per month / week / day, and your bounce rate. **They are only going to pay you if your target market is what they're after and if they can get a good return on investment.** They are not going to pay you if you have three subscribers and no readers. Okay? Okay. You must build a brand. It takes time to build those numbers. Full stop.

- **Same goes for ad space**. If you're selling some ad space on your site, the same information applies. You need good metrics. You need a good audience.
- **Affiliate ads**. I know that affiliate ads are a big deal. There are all sorts of click-bait plug-ins that promise to pay you for hosting their ads. Hell, if you have an Amazon affiliate account, you can create an ad box that will populate. Here's the deal with those. You have practically no control over what shows up. If you're all family-friendly and wholesome (and there is nothing wrong with that, by the way), you can't control the ads that pop up promising that someone's fake boob cream is the "Kardashian secret" to modeling fame. You can't control it if erotica books or sex toys start popping up in your Amazon ads. I've seen this happen to friends. And with the affiliate ads? I hope you have good traffic. And that they like clicking spam links. And that they stay on those sites. Because that's the only way you're going to earn your pennies in hopes of a payout. With Amazon, if someone uses your affiliate link and makes a purchase you do get a smidge of money. I have a friend who has an Amazon affiliate account. She homeschools. I use her affiliate link all the time when I buy stuff so that she gets a cut of the money. But you can't necessarily expect your friends or family to remember to do that...or even that they will do that. People are lazy.
- **Some audiences find monetization to be sketchy**. Even if you use a disclaimer that says an ad is sponsored and you promise to still give your honest opinion, that doesn't mean your readers will believe you. Many find affiliate links to Amazon more honest and preferable. I visit a lot of recipe / cooking sites. Those are quite common. However, they're also not embedded all over the place.

- **Too many ads can slow down your page loading time.** We live in the ADD generation. Loading speed is important. If it takes too long for your page to load or has too many ads, your people are going to bounce.

Content Creation Strategy

To create good content, you must spend time thinking about what your target audience wants. You must also stay on top of research as to what others in your space are doing.

Take some time each week to think about content. You can create an editorial calendar if you want. This can be monthly or weekly. You can make it for the whole year. You can make it for a quarter. The purpose of an editorial calendar is to give you a place to write down your content ideas and create a schedule you'll use for publication. For example, if you choose a biweekly editorial plan, maybe you publish on the 1st and 15th. If you want to publish once a week, maybe you publish on Tuesdays. (Of course, as time goes on, you'll see your blog stats and you can adjust your days accordingly. Currently, my most popular reader day is Thursday at 1 pm! It started off as Tuesdays around 3 am.)

Okay, so let's talk about some basic types of content. Evergreen content is ripe for sharing over and over again (not spamming every ten minutes!). It's content that doesn't really change with time. For example, how to get content ideas when you have no idea what you're really doing. Ultimately, you may develop your own methods...but my basic methods don't change over time. I teach them over and over again. They get you through until you find your own rhythm.

Then, there's dated content. There is nothing wrong with dated content particularly if what you're sharing is newsworthy for your industry. I've written about lawsuits, changes in the law, politicians getting sued, current business trends, and the likes. You know, things that change. I don't necessarily just summarize what happened. Instead, I try to make it relevant to my audience...like giving them a lesson.

A lot of people refer to this as "newsjacking." And there is a right and a wrong way to do newsjacking. I'll summarize the wrong way to newsjack: stealing someone's entire article instead of just linking to it.

The right way to newsjack: write a good headline and then write a good introduction that links to the original article. Then, take the key points of the article and discuss how it can affect your audience. I wrote about the pros and cons of newsjacking on my blog. The pros:

- It's not a new concept. Opinion pieces have always existed. We just gave opinion pieces a new name that doesn't exactly sound all that nice.
- It can get a regular audience to your site. No matter how niche your audience is, they don't want to read the same content all the time. When you take certain newsworthy items and make them interesting and applicable to your audience (without offending them), you get more readers and likely more shares. This can also be a con to newsjacking. You can piss people off and they might unsubscribe. Choose your pieces carefully.
- You get a good opportunity to piggyback off of something newsworthy and hopefully go viral. Link out to good, reputable sites. Mention the author of the original article on Twitter. Let them know you linked to them if you wrote about the piece without criticizing the author. If they like what you did, they

may share it out. They may also want to work with you in the future.
- It's an easy strategy you can use when you really don't know what to write about.

Sounds great, doesn't it? But like anything that includes opinion and analysis, it's not all sunshine and roses. This is the Internet-age. Someone will be offended. I don't go out of my way to offend anyone, especially when I'm projecting a business persona. I try to keep my newsjacking analytical. Yet, it still happens. So, here's the list of potential consequences:

- If you're not careful, you can alienate your audience...especially if you are the brand. I know, everyone wants to be all politically motivated and a right-fighter. That's cool, but be careful about alienating your audience. If you look me up online, you'll find articles I've written about news and politics. You'll notice, though, that they're not subversive. Also, on the rare occasions I choose to engage someone with a different opinion, I use facts. I don't name call. Ever. Getting political is bad for business (unless you're in the business of politics or maybe civil rights law).
- If you write something that pisses off the general public, you could go viral. And you probably won't enjoy it. Just because you can say it, doesn't mean you should. And you're certainly not immune from the fallout of running your mouth. Also, slander and libel are very real legal charges. And someone with money could make them stick to you and shut you down. Be honest. Be careful.
- It's dated. You might not be able to share it much.

Alright, moving on in content strategy, let's talk about other sites in your industry. As you learned earlier, I don't believe in the concept of competition. The word competition comes from the Latin word "competere" which means to strive together. Established businesses in your industry are a goldmine when it comes to content. No, you're not going to steal their work and claim it as your own. Ever. First, you're going to complete a basic Internet search. For example, if you're a small business accountant in Texas, you'd search on just that: small business accountant in Texas.

Not counting the ads at the top of pages one and two, I want you to make a list (Evernote is good for this. You can also just use a Word document) of the top websites that come up with those search terms. We'll get back to those soon.

Next, as you scroll through the first page of results, look for search results that look like they're written in a Q/A style. Look at those. Are they questions that your target audience may have? Hint: Most of the time, yes. Sometimes, you'll get some weird ones that don't fit, but most of the time they are really good questions. Write down the best questions.

Scroll to the bottom of page one. What are the suggested or recommended searches? Which of those could you theoretically see your clients using? Write those down.

Now, I want you to take a few minutes and review the Q/As the first two pages of interesting links that popped up, and the suggested searches. Draw a line underneath all of that info if you're writing this out by hand or start a new page in your Word document. I want you to jot down five to ten ideas that you think your target market would want to know. There's no right or wrong answer.

You can refine those terms by going to Google and typing (one at a time) those new ideas. As you type, look at what pops up underneath. Do any of those look like really good ideas? Write those down, too. Hit enter on the first term.

Look at what pops up, and the Q/As, and the suggested searches. Maybe write down the ones that really stand out.

When you've had enough of this activity, we're going to move on to looking at some of the domains or blogs you found on the first couple of pages of results.

You want to look at a few things on each one. The overall ease of navigating their site, whether they have a FAQ, and some of the pages they have related to their services. Of course, you want to find their blog or "news" page. I have found it is easiest to open the FAQ page and blog / new page in separate tabs. With the FAQ page, read over the questions that are asked and how they are answered. Chances are, they look like very basic questions...and that's okay. You do not have to reinvent the wheel. You have no way to know where a page visitor is in their research or knowledge about what you do. It's important to cover the basics in a way that is friendly and easy to understand. Don't talk down to your potential clients. Don't talk over their heads. Be professional, but be polite. The FAQ page can inspire you for your own version and also for blog posts. What FAQ questions are listed that you think you could turn into a blog post? Write that topic down.

Move on to the blog page. What sort of topics do they post about? You may or may not see any comments. That could be for a couple of reasons. They may not have their blog enabled for comments. They may not have any interaction. Business blogs don't always get a lot of interaction in the commenting sense unless they are news focused. Even then, it may be hit or miss depending on the focus and the traffic. Out of the topics you find on their blog, which ones can you write about on your own? Which ones can you expand on?

Now, with all of the information you've looked at, take a few more minutes to think. What other topics could you write about?

Turn your attention back to your editorial calendar. Begin putting your favorite ideas onto your calendar. Remember, planning is great, but it does you no good if you don't take action.

By the way, there are online tools that exist (the best ones cost money...not necessarily a lot of money...but some are quite costly) that can tell you the best keywords from any domain, their most visited blog posts or pages, and the likes. This can be a great tool to gain an edge, but it's really not necessary in the beginning.

Email Lists and Digital Downloads

I have mixed feelings on email lists. I have one. I don't use it. If I don't use it, why do I have one? Initially because I thought I would use it for marketing. I thought I would use it to sell books or courses or whatever. Then, having it just sort of morphed into learning how to write good email copy and how to use MailChimp. By the way, there are a lot of email list building companies that have free accounts or low-cost accounts. Start with the free account.

Building an email list can take time. You can use it for a lot of different purposes. You can even build different sorts of email lists. Maybe you have one that is for certain industries that want one specific service. Maybe you have another for current clients. Maybe you have a special list for special occasions. Segmentation is important.

People should be able to sign up for your email list, if you're going to use one, on your website. Don't be annoying. They do not need a popup every five seconds on every page they visit. People will bounce. Choose an opt-in tool that will help you and think about your own likes and dislikes. You can also use Wix or Weebly to build a landing page where people go specifically to sign up for your newsletter. I use Wix for that.

Whatever you're sending out, make sure it's valuable content. No one wants a constant sales job despite what you hear. Share your knowledge. I promise you're not taking work away from yourself. It showcases what you can do. It showcases how helpful you can be. Most people will not act on those tips on their own. Instead, they will learn to appreciate what's involved in what you do and they will hire you. I created a book for lawyers about SEO basics. The goal was to educate lawyers so that they could either do their own basic SEO work on a simple website **or** they could hold a conversation with an SEO "expert" (I use the term loosely because there are a lot of people out there who really don't know what they're doing) and understand if that person can meet their needs and so that they can ask good questions. As of 2018, the first edition (I really need to update and expand the book) was approximately four and a half years old. That's really old for some SEO trends (but I talked about basics like choosing keywords and terms they should understand). To this day, the book is still being purchased on Amazon. I still get emails from lawyers asking to hire me after reading the book. An old book. They have the knowledge. They don't have the time or the desire to DIY it.

One way that many people grow their email list is by providing some sort of free digital download (and, yes, there are people who also create paid digital content). Most people are extremely possessive of their email addresses. You know what it's like to get unwanted spam. You also know what it's like to sign up for a newsletter to get some sort of freebie and then being underwhelmed.

If you're creating a digital download, make sure it's something your audience really wants. Again, it's about showcasing your knowledge. Think about the things that will cause your clients to seek you out. What problems do you solve? How do those problems really affect your clients? You can create mini-guides on dealing with those problems. As a content strategist and writer, my clients want to know about how they can get more people to their blog or website in the hopes of converting them to paid clients (which is best done by showing off your knowledge and how you solve problems for your clients). I have a paid course on how someone can find the best keywords and how to write blogs. I could use that and create a more barebones version to give away if I wanted to grow an email list. Because that's why people hire me: content.

Regardless of what you create or what you want ultimately want to do with an email address, I have one piece of advice for you. Don't spam people. Use a drip campaign if you're getting people to sign up to your mailing list with a "free course on _____." A drip campaign will send out emails on their own. Again, make sure it is information clients actually want. Don't be too broad. Show and share your knowledge. Do the research and know how often you should email your list. Look for articles written by reputable sources that explain to you the best way to create email subjects that get people to open (don't use the word "free" because that triggers most spam filters particularly if you're not whitelisted). Read about the best way to construct an email that will get your list members to take action. And always include a call to action.

Finally, think about some of the email lists you've belonged to in the past or that you belong to now. What made you want to sign up? How often do you actually open the emails sent to you? If you marked them as spam or unsubscribed, why? Think about what you like and what you don't like…and think about your potential clients.

Productivity Isn't the Same as Busyness

This is another one of those parts of the book that probably won't win me any friends, but it's an absolute necessity. You must learn the difference between busy work and truly being productive. This is often difficult in the beginning because literally everything about your business is on your shoulders. You must do the planning and the execution of everything. It's up to you to write proposals, take care of marketing, and interact with potential clients. It's also up to you to handle any project that you win.

But…there's a still difference between being productive and being busy. Do you really need to tweak your website for the 600,000,005th time before you finally launch it? Probably not. It's an internal fear you haven't faced. You're worried people won't like it. Launch the damn thing. You can fix problems as they arise. I do that all the freaking time on my personal blog. I launched it. I post fairly regularly. I also get messages and emails about various little typos. And most of the time, I don't go back and fix the typos. That's a side project. It's not a book. It's not a project that makes me any money. I'm not out for perfection. Perfection is great, but it kills our ability to take action.

Looking at your email for the 908th time in the last ten minutes doesn't make you productive. It makes you a procrastinator. Turn off your notifications. Shut your email. Work through the boredom and the anxiety. Work when you're unsure. Do the work. There's no real way around these feelings. They happen. Period. The sooner you train yourself to work through them, the sooner it stops happening so often.

Taxes

Okay, first things first. I am not a tax expert. Yes, you need to pay your taxes. Yes, how you incorporate (or if you incorporate) changes how you may file your taxes. For example, if you create an LLC, you'll use a couple of extra schedules as well as your traditional 1040. Yes, you must report your taxes to the state and to the federal government. Here are my top tips to prepare you for tax season:

- **Separate out your personal finances from your business finances.** Pay yourself out of your business account.
- **Keep accurate bank records.** Keep accurate financial records in general…and keep an eye on any and all of your bank accounts.
- **Keep receipts.** There are all kinds of great write-offs. Again, I am not a tax expert. You should talk to a CPA about your business and what would count as a write-off for you. Not every meal you eat means you get to write it off. Yet, there are certifications, courses, ink pens, laptops, software choices, etc., that make great write-offs.
- **If you make more than $600 from any one client, they must provide you with a 1099M by the end of February.** That is, of course, unless you have a client that writes off what they pay you in another way. I have one or two that write me off as a marketing expense. I still have to pay taxes on what they pay.
- **Use some sort of accounting software to help you keep track of what you're making and spending.** There are lots of great choices that are easy to use

and affordable. QuickBooks is always an option. Zoho Invoicing is an easy to use option. You might want to choose a software that not only allows you to keep up with your business finances but that also allows you to track time, create invoices, and accept online payments.
- **Hire a CPA at tax time.** And provide them with all of your finance records for your business. That's another good reason to use something like QuickBooks or Zoho. It makes it easy to give your CPA everything they need to do your taxes. Don't look at this as an expense. Look at it as an investment into your peace of mind. Your CPA can do more than help you with your taxes. They may also be able to help you get and maintain financial control over your entire life.

Should I Sign That?

As a small business owner, you should have certain forms on hand to use with clients and even subcontractors (or employees). You may also be asked to sign certain things. In this section, you're going to learn a little bit about some of the most common forms involves in small business ownership and what you should look for before you sign or use the document. Why the latter? Because there are a lot of free forms out there...but that doesn't mean that they're any good! The following aren't listed in any particular order.

Independent Contractor Agreement. If you're going to hire independent contractors in the future instead of hiring employees, you need an independent contractor agreement. This agreement specifies that the person you're working with is not your employee (or that you aren't their employee). It outlines the name and scope of the project, deadlines involved, documents rate of pay and when payment will occur, should include the duties of both parties, the reasons why the contract or agreement may be terminated, and the state that will govern the agreement. The document should be signed by both parties. Sometimes, an independent contractor agreement may contain other clauses such as a confidentiality clause or a non-compete clause. Read those clauses carefully before you sign the document

Non-Compete Agreement. This may also be a clause in another contract. There are a couple of things to keep in mind. Many states limit non-compete agreements because they've been abused in the past. Most states have a law that regulates how long a non-compete agreement or clause may be used. This clause or agreement limits the signing party from doing certain types of work or jobs or working within a certain demographic or industry for a certain amount of time. Of course, my non-compete is way simpler. I just limit those signing it from pursuing my clients for the maximum amount of time in my state.

Non-Disclosure Agreement. This is a stand-alone agreement that may also be used as a clause in a contract. It basically states that whatever processes or procedures someone is exposed to over the course of a project they may not tell others about for a certain amount of time. This could include the use of customized software, business practices, current projects, and future projects.

If you're working in a creative capacity and you come up with a new invention, program, or even a new workflow process, you need to know ahead of time who will own your idea, invention, or program. This is extremely important. If you don't protect your intellectual property before you sign any contract, you could lose the ability to use or take your designs with you when the project is complete.

If you have any questions at all about anything you're asked to sign, have the agreement reviewed by a lawyer. If you're looking to purchase a basic independent contractor agreement for future use, I recommend FormSwift, US Legal Forms, or LegalZoom. Whatever form, where ever you get it from, should be state specific. You can also pay a lawyer to draft one with your best interests in mind that you can continue to use in the future.

Finally, be open and honest before signing anything about whether you'd like to use some or all of the project for your portfolio. Many clients are amicable to this. If they are, those allowances should be mentioned within any agreement before you sign it.

Conclusion

Honestly, there's so much more I could continue to write about. There are tons of other marketing ideas that are free or low cost. There are tons of business practices and designs I could discuss. However, at around 33,000 words, that's probably more than enough to get you started.

So go out there, kill something, and drag it home!

---

[1] https://www.sba.gov/sites/default/files/advocacy/SB-FAQ-2016_WEB.pdf

---

[i] Philippians 4:12
[ii] https://www.entrepreneur.com/article/227990

[iii] https://www.scientificamerican.com/article/dress-for-success-how-clothes-influence-our-performance/

www.ingramcontent.com/pod-product-compliance
Lightning Source LLC
Chambersburg PA
CBHW051321220526
45468CB00004B/1451